Drawn & Engraved by T. Taylor, at J.M. Butler's establishment, 242 Chestnut St Philad.ª

THE WHITEFIELD HOUSE

SKETCHES

OF

MORAVIAN LIFE

AND

CHARACTER.

COMPRISING

A GENERAL VIEW OF THE HISTORY, LIFE, CHARACTER, AND RELIGIOUS AND EDUCATIONAL INSTITUTIONS OF THE UNITAS FRATRUM.

BY JAMES HENRY.

MEMBER OF THE MORAVIAN HISTORICAL SOCIETY, AND OF THE HISTORICAL SOCIETY OF PENNSYLVANIA.

PHILADELPHIA:
J. B. LIPPINCOTT & CO.
1859.

CONTENTS.

MORAVIAN LIFE AND CHARACTER.

I.

INTRODUCTION.

IN presenting a picture of Moravian life, exemplified by certain portions of its history and biography, my object has been to furnish such an æsthetic view of the subject as might be likely to draw the attention of those who have either not been observers, or have formed misconceptions of it.

To the many who search out greatness in the numerical strength, eclat, and general worldly influence of a people, it may appear a matter of wonder why the Brethren's Church should be at all deserving of a place in history; since the space it occupies in society is so small, the influence it wields so unpopular, and the decorations of its exterior worship so little in accordance with the sensuous wants of the times we live in, as well as of all time. The only answer to this is, that the existence of the people called United Brethren is a great historical fact, in the present and the past. Regarding the term in its

2

purest sense, it is certainly one of the oldest Christian peoples living; and it will be my aim to show in these Sketches that, though almost crushed at times by civil and ecclesiastical power, it was never annihilated. Its great age and its remarkable tenacity of spiritual life, its striking powers of endurance under the hand of brute force, render it worthy of a name, and that name is no small one in the world's history.

A characteristic trait in Moravianism, old as well as new, has been its entire independence of all the palpable extraneous aid that gives the dominant religions, and more particularly the Roman Catholic faith, their greatest popular strength. In early times it knew but little of churches; the old Bohemians and Moravians were wont to worship in secrecy, and even in the times of the newly-arisen church, the sanctuary was a place of no architectural attraction, but a simple room in some appropriate dwelling.

That the elements of this Christian people could never assimilate with the great worldly element, is, perhaps, its chosen and distinctive feature; the beauty that adorns its whole historical life. All its associations, as read in the hymns of Zinzendorf, and heard in the tones of its music, are unworldly and distasteful to the multitude; and hence the Brethren remained a small Christian family, and ever will remain such, if their ritual be preserved pure, uncorrupted, and savored with apostolic simplicity.

Since the first renewal of the United Brethren's Church in 1722, it met with opposition and prejudice wherever it worked its way, in civilized as well as uncivilized society, and the history of its progress through all obstacles forms a curious as well as an interesting portion of the biography of Zinzendorf and his compeers.

The works which have emanated from Moravian minds are quite numerous, and relate to doctrines, synods, general Moravian history, memoirs of eminent men, sermons, hymns, essays, missions, and, occasionally, a religious fiction. The larger proportion of these writings are the production of German Brethren; some very important ones are English, and a few American.

In reference to the opposition met with by the Renewed Brethren's Church, I would add that numerous writers have appeared from time to time, sending their shafts of censure and misinterpretation against it, and covering with obloquy the simple institutions that grew up in Herrnhut. The works of the enemy form quite a little library in the archives of that place, and are carefully preserved by our people themselves; while on the opposite side of the same apartment are ranged all those volumes that were written in their defence or commendation.

All this literature, for and against Moravianism, had its origin in a country where thought is active, and the human mind unfathomable;—where reason and faith are diverging to opposite extremes. While the former is seen to cast off all the hopes and aspirations that foreshadow an unseen world, rending asunder man's relations with an endless life, and making his emotional being only subservient to the purposes of his sensual existence, the latter enters more deeply into religion, thinks more intensely *upon* and *within* it, and calls out more of its essential beauty, than the faith of any other country on earth is capable of conceiving.

Zinzendorf was not the first to pave the way for an evangelical church, such as his institutions presented to the world, for Spener and Franke went before him. The former was born in 1635, and died in 1705. His theatre of action was chiefly at Frankfort-on-the-Main; he carried his doctrines among all classes, amid the cottages of the peasant and the palaces of the noble. He wrote the "*Pia Desideria;*" and Zinzendorf's eulogy upon him was, "Spener was a child of God, and this was more than all his other gifts, his learning and his high offices."

Franke, a student of Spener's, was born in 1662, was formed in his school of religious thought, and received an appointment in the University of Halle. There, with seven guilders, he commenced an orphan-house, out of which grew up the world-renowned Orphanotrophy of Halle. His favorite motto was, "Pray and labor;" and his popularity spread throughout Germany. He died in 1727.

At the time of his own appearance there, Zinzendorf found Germany and other parts of Europe favorable to the reception of his simple doctrines; and most of the opposition to him seems to have been grounded upon information about him and the community at Herrnhut, conveyed through improper channels. His whole scheme was so original, the new character assumed by the nobleman in descending from titles and estates to pursue life among all men promiscuously, in forsaking the gayeties of a court and going back to the apostolic age for his ideal of a modern association, formed so strange a phenomenon, that many doubted the rationality of the whole proceeding.

But notwithstanding all the writing to which this new and singular spectacle gave rise, Moravianism grew apace; Germany, Denmark, Switzerland, England and America welcomed and adopted it, not among indiscriminate masses in cities, but generally in villages built up by its own people, and used as their exclusive dwelling-places.

In the Sketches of Moravian life itself, as given in the following pages, much has reference to the past, as, in consonance with a new order of things, new men, and new ideas, we are willing that a great deal that was old and long cherished should become obsolete, and that life should come up under new forms.

In our European congregations our Brethren are more tenacious of their birth-right; they have forsaken little they once possessed, and live in isolated villages; but whether the infection of European society and all its social dangers is destined to invade them at some future day, it is not in my province to predict. Zinzendorf himself never saw such a distant future before him, when he planted his standard in Lusatia, and sung, that "as long as it remained held within the bonds of love, as long as the work of its Master was unmolested, so long should Herrnhut firmly stand:"

"Herrnhut soll nicht länger stehen
Als die Werke deiner Hand
Ungehindert drinnen gehen
Und die Liebe sey sein Band," etc.

He then would scarcely have conceived that the influences and practices instituted around the Hutberg were to extend among 200,000 people, as our statistics inform us they do at the present day.

From our own stand-point in society it is pleasant to look back upon the scenes of which I have here attempted some feeble outlines. It may justly be said that Paris and its influences govern the whole civilized world. In this, our favored country, all the corruptions, the superficial tone, the attire, the seductions and the glare of society take their impress from the centre of what is falsely termed refinement, and in placing this refinement side by side with that of the older Moravian, we shall discover the emptiness of a materialistic life and the never-fading beauty of an inner one.

But in doing away with old things, that have once been rooted in the affections of man, we seldom see them utterly destroyed. Obsolete forms are always coming up again, old costumes are adapted and applied to the tastes of the age, and many antique models of architecture are resuscitated. The games of the youth of many generations gone by are the games of the living, and the songs of the past are sung over again. In the history of the human heart and the clothing of its affections there is *no progress*, and we cannot tear it away from its old images without finding it recurring to them again.

The hardest struggle man has to encounter is with the world *as it is*, and the highest point of moral power he can ever attain to, is to be emancipated from all its influences and think for himself. Firmly stationed on that pedestal of original thought, his teachings reach far into futurity, and he is felt long after those who had opposed him have become forgotten and unknown. The sentiment applies to Zinzendorf, both as an apostle and an original thinker; as to one endowed with Christian zeal, and persisting in independence of thought. As a man classed among the worldly great, but not in the same category with human greatness in its outer brilliancy, he is still known in Germany, for his marble statue stands in the Valhalla of Bavaria.

II.

THE ANCIENT UNITAS FRATRUM.

In extending our researches into the obscurity of the Old Brethren's Church, we shall find that Bohemia and Moravia formed the ground of its development and greatest activity.

The inhabitants of that portion of Europe were, perhaps, more tenacious of their religious faith than any other cotemporary races, and all the vicissitudes that distinguish their annals, all their wars and persecutions, arose from that remarkable spiritual principle which inspired them throughout the long, slowly advancing centuries of that medieval period of modern history. These peoples claimed an ancestry from the Sclavonic nations, among whom Christianity had found its way during some of the first centuries, but left no visible fruits until about the ninth century, which is regarded as the great epoch of conversion among them.

It was then that we hear of two Greek monks, Cyrillus and Methodius, entering, with the inculcations of Christ in their apostolic purity, into Bohemia and Moravia, although, as just observed, Christianity had found access there at a much more remote day. After their appearance, all those divisions of the church which had fallen off from their allegiance to the Roman See joined the newly-converted Sclavonic races; but its inquisitorial power was soon at work, and took hasty and decisive steps to counteract the defection and show its opposition to the spread of the Greek faith by edicts, persecution, and imprisonment.

The Bohemians and Moravians became, thenceforth, the marked objects of papal rancor; but it is a notable circumstance in the annals of these Christians, that no political or hierarchical authority could ever crush them or force them to renounce the forms of belief and worship that had their foundation in the authentic scriptural records which they sacredly preserved.

As early as the tenth century, Pope John XIII. had compelled the Bohemians and Moravians to exchange the Greek for the Latin worship, but this compulsion was only of transient effect, and they soon shook off their new creed. Persecution now assailed them in its greatest virulence, but they encountered it with a degree of heroïsm that characterized them up to the close of the seventeenth century, soon after which we find their last remnants emigrating to Lusatia and joining Zinzendorf.

Prague was made the seat of a Roman episcopacy,

Dithmar, of Magdeburg, installed as bishop, and the Roman liturgy introduced. The Bohemians sent deputies to Rome in the year 977, desiring the use of their native language in religious services. This they were permitted to enjoy in some small degree only, and finally, when it was interdicted, a large portion of them fell off from Romanism and worshiped in private. Pope Gregory VII. or Hildebrand, at the close of the eleventh century, issued a severe edict against them, which was supported by force; and this forms the point in their history which was most distinguished by papal oppression, and where the scenes of unmitigated cruelty are most plainly visible.

The Church of Rome became sensibly more and more degenerate, and as it departed from the pure faith of the apostolic times into the mazes of error, the Sclavonic people shrunk within their homes and made their sanctuaries in secret places. Their days of oppression lasted through the lapse of more than a century; they restricted themselves, during all this gloomy period, to their own Greek forms and rituals as well as they could; but new dangers now presented themselves before them in the shape of corruption in their internal constitution and practices. From this jeopardy they seem to have been rescued by a remarkable providential interposition, which was a union with several new contemporary Christian sects, who came hither from different quarters of Europe and espoused their cause. For now the Waldenses, a pure and primitive people, made their appearance in Bohemia, (Anno 1176,) settled along the borders of the Eger, and soon became united in friendly and religious communion with the Bohemians and Moravians. Their early history is involved in uncertainty, some dating their origin in the eighth or ninth century, while others seek for it long prior to that time. They inhabited the valleys of Piedmont and France, and received their appellation either from Peter Waldo or from their being Valdesi, or inhabitants of the valley.

The Waldenses are looked upon as the earliest champions of Christian truth, but its advocacy brought upon them the most relentless persecution, followed, during the thirteenth century, by numerous cases of martyrdom. But, notwithstanding this, they spread, and though during the ascendency of the Bohemians and Moravians they dwindled into a small band of people, their descendants are found to this day in the valleys of Piedmont, Switzerland, and Southern France. They traced their episcopal ordination to the Apostles, and when they arrived in Bohemia they found their doctrines and practices to assimilate with those of the uncorrupted Christians of that country. During the fourteenth century the Wickliffites made their appearance on the stage of church history, and they, like all other reformers, had to endure the enmity, reproach, and tortures of papal intolerance and power. It is not probable that John Wickliffe went personally to Bohemia, but it is known that his followers emigrated thither, circulated his writings and doctrines, and finally, merged into the Brethren's Church.

The Hussites sprung from the Bohemian, John Huss, professor of an academy, and, in 1400, its preacher in Prague, who was uniform in his doctrines and professions with his predecessors, the Waldenses and Wickliffites. In consequence of the fearlessness he showed in promulgating evangelical truths, the imprecations, threats, and denunciations of Rome were showered upon him. He traveled, under the feigned protection of the Emperor Sigismund, to Constance, to appear before the council, where he was condemned as a heretic, and on the sixth of July, 1415, surrendered his life at the stake, with that remarkable equanimity which has rendered his name one of the most prominent in the history of martyrdom. The result of this sacrifice was the war of the Hussites, commenced by the rebellious Bohemians, under their leader Zisca, or John of Trautenau, and continued ten years after his death.

A portion of these Bohemians contended chiefly for the restoration of the sacramental chalice, and were thence called Calixtines; the more quiet and prudent of them, however, held their meetings upon a mountain, to which Zisca gave the name of Mount

Tabor, whence they derived the appellation of Taborites.

During the whole time of their association with these various sects, the Bohemians and Moravians remained the object of odium to the Church of Rome, and its emissaries were ever at work to reduce them to obedience, or entice them to the observance of its own worship and to renounce their purer faith. But although they could not emancipate themselves from this reign of spiritual oppression, still they conducted their worship in secret places, and often in caves, whence they obtained the name of "Speluncales," until, finally, in the middle of the fifteenth century, King George Podiebrad showed them so much leniency as to permit them to settle in the Principality of Litiz, on the borders of Moravia; and, in the year 1456, they formed themselves into the association of the Unitas Fratrum, at Kunewald. Their security here was but short-lived, for in a few years afterwards King Podiebrad himself sanctioned a violent persecution against them, in which the Calixtine priests and the Romish clergy were implicated. The Brethren were expelled from their villages, many were imprisoned, and others driven to the stake. But, notwithstanding all this, they met together in solitudes, enacted new regulations, and their government was entrusted to elders, who were chosen by ballot. They increased in numbers, received accessions from among the most distinguished Bohemians and Moravians, as well as from strangers, and even held synods among the recesses of the mountains.

In the year 1467 a deputation from the Bohemian and Moravian Brethren met in synod at Lhota, consisting of seventy of the most reputable of their people. Nine of these, of the most undoubted character, were chosen, from among whom three were selected by lot to constitute their priests and spiritual advisers. These three men were Matthias of Kunewald, Thomas Przelaucius, and Elias Krenovius. Having, in a subsequent synod, discussed the question whether the elders, who were called presbyters among the Apostles and early Christians, could perform the office of ordination as well as the bishops, it was decided that such a rule was, in all respects, conformable to the example of the primitive church and to the writings of the early fathers. They reasoned upon this authority that their presbyters might, very properly, administer the rites of ordination; but, in order to meet all the objections of their opponents, they decided upon seeking episcopal ordination from some pure source, and, accordingly, turned their attention to the Waldenses, whose history showed an uninterrupted line of episcopacy connected with that of apostolic times.

The Waldenses still had their churches and bishops in Austria, and our Brethren decided upon sending thither three of their priests, one of whom was Michael Bradacius, to receive this sacred anointment from the last remaining of the Waldensian bishops, Stephen. He hailed the Brethren with warmth, rejoiced to hear of the Christian life among them, presented them in detail the whole history of his church, its long array of bishops, and then imparted to the three men the rite of episcopal ordination.

Hardly a year had elapsed after this event before the Brethren were again assailed by their enemies. Their friends, the Waldenses, had passed through an equally severe ordeal in Austria, and their bishop, Stephen, who had been the instrument of transmitting the episcopacy to the Brethren, and thence to our present church, was burned, and his people scattered in dismay. The prisons of Bohemia were filled with the devoted victims of our ancient church, where many were starved to death, and other equal horrors imposed upon them.

The Bohemian crown now descending upon the head of Wladislaus of Poland, a prince of mild disposition, the Brethren were allowed an opportunity of recovering their lost privileges, and once more enjoying their religion, and they were so far restored to comparative ease and security, that in the year 1500 they numbered two hundred congregations in Bohemia and Moravia.

In 1508 the Bohemian king was prevailed upon by the Roman clergy to sign an edict against the Brethren, with that subserviency which other potentates had shown to the power of Rome, for scarcely had he closed the transaction than he fell on his knees, in the presence of the bishops who had led him into its performance, and prayed to God that the edict might not be fulfilled. The scenes of former years, however, followed; the Bohemians were martyred and burned; they fasted and prayed, and, finally, turned their thoughts toward forsaking their country altogether. With this view they decided that four of their number should depart, separately, into foreign lands, on the errand of seeking out a new people, who were living in the practice of a pure faith, and knew the true God, with whom they might join themselves. The first member of this little embassy proceeded to Greece, the second to Russia, the third to Thrace and Bulgaria, and the fourth to Palestine and Egypt. When these men returned home, they reported to their countrymen that the people they had sought could nowhere be found; that the world, as they had everywhere beheld it, was corrupt and fallen, and the so-called Christians sunk in superstition.

They next sent messengers in search of the Waldenses, hoping to find some remnant of these in France and elsewhere, with whom they might possibly form a renewed friendship and communion. But of the Waldenses a mere handful was found still existing, in scattered abodes, and the Brethren had to resign themselves to their forlorn condition, and pray for the coming of some great reformer, whose name might be the signal of a general regeneration of the Christian church.

During that time the art of printing added its facilities to the publication and dissemination of the Scriptures, and the Bohemian Brethren, who had translated them into their own language, issued the Bible in Venice, which went through two subsequent editions in Nuremberg. They, at the same time, opened a correspondence with Erasmus, of Rotterdam, who ratified all they had written and spoken in self-defence, but advised them to proceed in their worship in quiet and reserve; he commended them for giving one another the appellation of brother and sister, admonished them to show less obedience to their preachers than to the Word of God, and put more trust in Him than in men.

A century had now elapsed since John Huss had uttered the remarkable prophecy to his persecutors: "In one hundred years, ye shall account to God and to me for what ye are now doing," when Luther arose in 1517, and attacked the errors of the ruling church by an exposure of all its notorious abuses. The advent of Luther was nowhere so gladly welcomed as among the down-trodden Bohemian and Moravian Brethren. They sent up their prayers to heaven at the prospect of a speedy rescue from thraldom and from the tortures of a bigoted and relentless enemy. In 1522 they deputed John Horn and Michael Weiss to wait upon Luther to bring him their kindly greetings, and congratulate him upon the great work he had assumed; to assure him of their co-operation in it, and uniting with this assurance the hope that the light of the true gospel might soon cast its refulgence over the nations of Europe. Luther's response was couched in the most friendly terms; he acknowledged the sincerity and earnestness of their love of the truth, and, at the same time, felt himself animated by such a noble example as their history and vicissitudes presented.

Both Luther and his coadjutor, Melanchthon, preserved the most amicable relations with the Unitas Fratrum, corresponded with them, received their repeated deputations, deliberated with them on church discipline and new reforms, the accomplishment of which was only frustrated by the termination of his heroic career. Before his death, the great reformer left a concise and expressive testimony in favor of the United Brethren in these memorable words: "Since the times of the Apostles no people have appeared who have made a nearer approach to them in faith and practice than the Bohemian Brethren. Although these Brethren do not excel us in purity of doctrine, since every point of our creed proceeds from the scriptural source, yet they are our superiors in church discipline, which dispenses the blessings of good government to their congregations; an acknowledgment which the love of truth and the glory of God exact from us."

Although the era of the Reformation had opened so promisingly to the United Brethren, they never realized the fulfillment of the hopes they had conceived in the appearance of Luther.

Their churches were again closed under the persecutions of government, and they were commanded either to unite themselves with the Church of Rome or forsake their country. In this extremity some joined the Calixtines, a few concealed themselves or dispersed in various directions, but the greater portion fled to Poland. Here their stay lasted but ten weeks, and they were once more driven out of the land, and fled to Prussia, where their creed underwent examination, and being found to correspond with all the articles of the Augsburg Confession, a number of towns were offered for their shelter and protection. Their exile here lasted until the mild government of Maximilian enabled them to enjoy their religion in their own country again, where we find them once more reinstated and holding synods in the year 1557, and in 1564 all their churches in Bohemia and Moravia were reopened for their use.

They now entered upon the task of a new translation of the Bible into the Bohemian language, and to effect this the more carefully and accurately, they sent students to the Universities of Wittemberg and Basle to learn the original languages. They established a press for the special purpose of its publication, and after fourteen years assiduous application, completed the Bohemian version, which afterwards went through several editions.

At the dawn of the seventeenth century the clouds of oppression once more lowered around the Brethren, and, in 1627, hundreds of nobles and burghers were forced to flee their country, and take refuge in Saxony, Silesia, Brandenburg, Poland, Prussia, Hungary, and elsewhere, and such as were not able to emigrate, remained the passive victims of papal tyranny, although no force or torture could drive them into its worship or allegiance.

From this date all evangelical religion seems to have been swept out of Bohemia and Moravia, and all their schools and churches were permanently closed. Every Bible that could be found, and all writings that tended to the diffusion of its doctrine, were industriously sought out and burned, and, by that striking perversion of the spirit and tendencies of Christ's mission on earth, which rendered hierarchical power so baneful to Europe, the lives and prosperity of thousands of exemplary and excellent men became a sacrifice.

Among those unfortunate exiles, the voice of one was heard to raise up in prayer during this hour of gloom, beseeching God to come to their rescue and restore to them their homes.

"We are orphans and are fatherless. Men persecute us; we labor and we have no rest. Servants have ruled over us; there is none that doth deliver us out of their hand. The joy of our heart has ceased; our dance is turned into mourning. But Thou, O Lord, remainest forever, and Thy throne endureth from generation to generation. Wherefore dost Thou forget us forever, and forsake us for so long a time? Lead us back to Thee again, so that we may again return home. Renew our days, as of old." (Lam. v.)

This Jeremiad proceeded from the lips of Amos Comenius, who was born at Canna, in Moravia, in 1592. He studied at Herborn, and, in 1614, returned home to his native country, and became a rector of the schools of Przerow, and distinguished himself ever afterwards for his profound knowledge in educational science. He was appointed pastor of the Unitas Fratrum at Fulneck, and assumed the superintendence of its schools. In 1621 this town was made a prey to the ravages of war, and the valuable library of Comenius plundered by the Spaniards. In 1624, when the edict was issued against all evangelical preachers of Bohemia and Moravia, Comenius took refuge in the mountains, and found protection under the Baron of Slaupna, during which time he instructed his children.

Some years afterwards he was obliged to escape with a portion of his congregation to Lissa, in Poland, where he continued his labors of instruction. In 1631 he published his famous work, "Janua linguarum reserata," which was translated into the German, Polish, Bohemian, Greek, English, French, Italian, Spanish, Dutch, Arabic, Turkish, Persian, and Mongolian languages. In 1638 his fame elicited for him an invitation to visit Sweden, to reform its school system; he concluded, however, to decline it, sending his advice and views on the subject to his friends in that country. In

1641 he received similar proposals from England, whither he actually went; but his plans for putting any new reforms into execution were frustrated by the civil war then prevailing. In 1642 he went to Sweden, and, rendering valuable services there in the cause of education, was rewarded with a pension, which was an ample competency for him, and enabled him to pursue his labors and writings in the same cause. His life, thus unremittingly devoted to literary and evangelical pursuits, finally closed at Hamburg, after he had reached the age of eighty years. In the year 1632 he had been chosen bishop of the Unitas Fratrum, and gave his daughter in marriage to Peter Jablonsky, subsequently bishop of the Brethren, and father of Daniel Ernest Jablonsky, through whom, as will be shown, the episcopal ordination was handed down to their renewed church.

At the close of the seventeenth and opening of the eighteenth centuries no distinct traces of the Unitas Fratrum are to be found in the countries of Bohemia and Moravia. After the peace of Westphalia all hope for them seems to have been lost, and they were, in consequence, obliged to hold themselves in more strict concealment than ever before. They escaped into other countries, where thousands sought and found protection. Some of these went to Prussia and Poland, but the majority to Saxony and Upper Lusatia. In Poland some of their congregation still survived, and many were induced to move thither and join them, but the larger portion of this ill-fated

Christian people by degrees became lost among other nations, and what once constituted the Ancient Unitas Fratrum was so entirely dispersed as to leave but few traces behind.

Of those few remnants of them, still lingering in Bohemia and Moravia, there were some who read the Bible in secret, even concealing it from their wives, children, and servants, and only availing themselves of the precepts it taught them, in instructing others. Their meetings were held in the night, and in cellars, or other unseen recesses; and wherever a few of them remained throughout the land, they pursued the practices and preserved the invincible fidelity to their religion, which had distinguished their forefathers for many centuries before them.

It was during this stage of the history of the Unitas Fratrum that the first movement took place in Lusatia, which attracted Christian David, the Nitschmanns, the Neisers, Toeltschig, Zeisberger and others to that hospitable region, where a safe asylum was held out to all who wished to enjoy the immunities and blessings of a pure evangelical worship. (See *Ratio Disciplinæ Unitatis Fratrum*, and *Lynar's Ursprung und Fortgange der Brüder Unität.*)

III.

HERRNHUT.

In that portion of eastern Saxony termed Upper Lusatia, or "Die Ober Lausitz," an old and beautiful country still greets the eye of the traveler. As he pursues the course of the "Chaussée," or public highway, running south from Loebau to Zittau, or, as he is more likely to do, takes that modern invention and destroyer of the poetical past, the locomotive, which now steams through the districts of country that have been the scenes of all the noted warfare of the last and the present century, from Charles XII. to Napoleon I., he will find himself cast among the varied associations of old Europe. Looking toward the south, the semicircular range of the Bohemian Mountains appears in view, rising here and there into those peculiar peaks which characterize the geology of this portion of the earth in contrast with our own. These form the boundary between Bohemia and Saxony, under the jurisdiction of the latter of which Lusatia still remains. To such a quiet and extremely aged picture as the landscape here furnishes, these mountains afford a most appropriate inclosure, and heighten, in a marked degree, the whole beauty of Lusatia. Scattered all around throughout this region are still to be found the vestiges of feudalism, and, occasionally, a cloister or a chapel. The ruins of the castle, where they yet exist, are carefully preserved with that veneration for the obsolete that results from a European education.

But what most strikes the American tourist, in these portions of central Europe, is the "Dorf" and its gray cottages. Many of these lowly structures may be centuries old, and are but in the earliest stage of their annals when our buildings reach their usual time of demolition. A dense thatch is seen to cover them, and the dark color and patches of moss that adorn it bespeak the degree of age that bears upon it. The homestead is comprised of a single building, the stable and dwelling being under one and the same roof. Aside of the low and narrow doorway is seen a small window, sufficient to afford a scanty supply of light, but pierced through walls of masonry that seem designed to last for ages. Within the dwelling-room itself, the most remarkable object is the huge tile-stone, occupying, in some smaller domiciles, nearly one-fourth of the apartment, and reaching up almost to the ceiling,—the top of it overhung with apparel, or covered with tools, cooking utensils, and a heterogeneous collection of the needful appointments of the household. In emerging from one of these venerable chambers, and casting an inquisitive glance upward, you will observe that a ladder, or some old, broken, and rickety stairs lead the way to the dormitory above. As there is never a fence, and seldom a hedge, either for the inclosure of field or garden, the cow, which constitutes one of the family's nearest neighbors, and occupies the same covering, is never seen in pasture; and the peasant is met coming in with a huge pile of fragrant clover, which he has just mown in the adjoining field. At almost every window in the larger-sized cottages a little projecting platform is covered with flower-pots, showing forth out of all the poverty of real life that feeling of poesy which ever reigns in pleasant companionship with nature herself,—with nature untrammeled by the adornments of false art, pure and expressive of simple joys.

Numerous are the pictures of living poetry in these antiquated lands; and when the stranger passes by or sojourns among them, he finds the original from which art has taken so many of her finest designs. It will not be required, nor indeed will it be well for him, to go into all the interior circumstances of life, as the comparison between its needful wants and actual supplies sometimes shows an appaling conclusion, and he might, perchance, fall into reflections which would mar all the beauty his imagination had aided him in raising up.

But it is not alone the exterior of life that should engage our attention here among these lowly homes. The human heart, as it lives and beats within them, is peculiarly constituted. To understand those hearts we must have access to their workings, by the medium of language, and that language is the one in which they are born, and live, and die.

When these people meet you, their greeting is that of affection. When the stranger from a distant land comes among them to seek out some remnants of an old ancestry, some long-forgotten ones, whose names have been handed down to him, he finds himself received with open arms and all the warmth of an old love. The words of welcome he finds addressed to him are significant of the most heartfelt joy. Such a model of moral beauty, springing out of humble life, the American is unaccustomed to, and in stepping aside from the great highway of travel among these rural abodes of Lusatia, he will be led into a comprehension of the nature, depth, and earnestness of the people from whom the Moravians have sprung.

In the midst of this country Herrnhut lies tranquil and undisturbed. Entering it from its northern side, over the "Chaussée," its quiet is so remarkable as to impress you with some unusual feeling. You greet and are greeted by every one of its inhabitants. The artisan seems hidden somewhere from notice, as the din of industry awakens but little attention and can scarcely be heard.

As you scan the environs of the village, nothing could present a more perfect idyl. Here the earth has no wastes; all its apportionments are perfectly garden-like, without even a hedge to show the demarkations of property.

In the picture of rural life, as here presented, there is a dreamy repose shed forth by the old ways, customs, pursuits, and external features of European inaction, that belongs only to itself and has no resemblance to life on this side of the Atlantic. But nature here is never purely herself; as the forest is planted, so the tree by the wayside is placed there by art; the woods are carefully culled of their exuberance, of their superfluous boughs, decayed limbs, or fallen trunks of trees, and the forest-keeper is a personage who figures everywhere. He plants and replants, and watches over these artificial groves, as the centuries fly along, leaving no such thing as native growth to be seen.

Of the objects that attract the visitor's attention, the "Hutberg" is the most prominent. This is an eminence in the upper portion of Herrnhut, on the slope of which the cemetery occupies a considerable space, surrounded and shaded by dense rows of lindens. Like all the other Moravian burial-places, the graves have their allotted portions of earth, and the name of the occupant is designated by inscriptions on small, oblong, and uniform marble slabs. An avenue of lindens leads from the village to the "Hutberg," beneath which the funeral procession passes when going from the church. Besides the solemn purposes to which it is applied, the cemetery is a thoroughfare, in strolling up to the summit of the "Hutberg" and to the observatory there, called the "Altan." The "Laube," or arbor, is found among its paths, where the pleasures of meditation are enjoyed in the vicinity of the grave. The peculiar poetry which the Moravian throws around the subject and circumstances of death, renders the combination of the arbor and the grave no incongruity, and you may often find these seats occupied by smiling and cheerful faces. A few flights of steps conduct to the summit of the "Hutberg," in emerging from the precincts of the burial-ground, and after having sought out the final resting-place of the most remarkable characters of Moravian history—such as Count Zinzendorf and the Countess, Anna Nitschmann, Christian David, Spangenberg, and many others, the first of whom has now reposed here nearly a century—you are tempted to seek the summit and look down on Herrnhut and its environs. Here the picture I have already attempted to describe becomes more panoramic, and, in addition to its varied and interesting features, the ancient village of Berthelsdorf attracts your attention.

Another long avenue, extending three-quarters of a mile from Herrnhut, and shaded by closely planted lindens, now very old and umbrageous, leads to Berthelsdorf, where are first observed two large buildings, occupied by ten members of the Unity's Conference and their families. This conference is to be considered as the ruling head and authority of the Moravian Church. In close proximity to these, stands the Manor House, or, at a later period, called the "Schloss,"[1] which, in its primitive form, was the family mansion of Count Zinzendorf, and was occupied by him as proprietor of the estates of Berthelsdorf during the infancy of Herrnhut, whither he removed subsequent to his marriage with the Countess Erdmuth Dorothea Reuss. On his final return thither, in 1757, he spent the remainder of his days in this mansion, where he died in 1760. At a later period the edifice was greatly enlarged, the improvements giving it the appearance of a "Schloss." It is now the residence of the President of the Unity's Conference and of other members thereof. Around an oval table in the second story are seen seated, three times each week, the Unity's Conference. Their time, during these sittings, which last from nine to half-past eleven o'clock in the morning, is chiefly devoted to the perusal of letters from every quarter of the globe. In these deliberations, Greenland, South Africa, Surinam, Australia, the West Indies, and North America, all come up in succession as subjects of consultation, and it constitutes the sole employment of the twelve members of this body to read and discuss measures growing out of this vast correspondence. No less than fifty letters per week are received

---

[1] Literally a castle, but the word applies to all structures of ample dimensions, and adapted to the uses of a large family mansion.

by the Conference from its various correspondents. The apartment which is the scene of these transactions is adorned with portraits of various Moravian characters, such as Zinzendorf, Spangenberg, Nitschmann, and Amos Comenius.

Passing somewhat farther down, from Herrnhut, and crossing a small brook, you enter the little hamlet of Berthelsdorf, and, proceeding among its extremely old and quaint homes, reach that ancient church, formerly used by Count Zinzendorf and Rothe, before the building of Herrnhut. It is now the village church of the Lutherans, and is the resort of the people in the vicinity. It is a remarkable edifice, having been founded five centuries ago, and is in excellent repair; it sends forth from within its adamantine walls, every Sabbath morn, the good old chorales of the Lutheran and Moravian Church. The edifice is larger than it originally was, having been renewed from time to time. It was fated to pass through many ordeals. In the war of the Hussites it was greatly injured by fire, and in 1538 the Roman Catholics were expelled from it and the priest driven out by main force. Berthelsdorf itself is situated in a valley, looking upward toward the "Hutberg," which rises 850 feet above the village. Its origin is wrapt in obscurity, and its name is supposed to have been derived from one Berthold, about the year 1346. It contains about 2000 inhabitants, and since 1480 has been in possession of the noble family of De Gersdorf.

A favorite resort of the inhabitants of Herrnhut is the "Heinrichsberg," a pleasure-ground among the beautiful ravines on one of the southern hillsides. Here numerous bowers and shady winding paths invite the young and old to spend the afternoon in the enjoyment of tea or coffee within their quiet recesses.

In giving a few of these characteristics of Herrnhut, as it now appears, my object is merely to introduce the subject of the following pages, by a presentation of the locality where Moravianism took its rise, and where it still flourishes, under the auspices of a small body of people who are imbued with its essential elements.

Of the company of Moravian exiles, the descendants of the old Bohemian and Moravian Church and of the original followers of John Huss, whose eventful history and claims to a pure episcopacy that pursued a stream uncontaminated by Popery from the apostolic ages, have just been told, Christian David was the most noted. He came to Berthelsdorf in company with his countrymen, espoused the cause of Zinzendorf, entered into the spirit of his plan for the erection of Herrnhut, and sedulously aided the designs of this new Christian apostle. The first tree felled for the purpose was close by the highway, and a "Denkmal," or monument, marks the spot, with a suitable inscription upon it describing the event. Around it are placed seats of stone, and this is a never-failing point of attraction to the historical visitor. Though 136 years have elapsed since that event, the original frame-work of Zinzendorf's spiritual system, conceived by himself and put into execution by his efforts, united with those of his followers, may still be regarded as perfect at Herrnhut.

In estimating the village system from its best point of view, we must regard with care the stress laid upon the organization of the congregation. Zinzendorf, whose genius was peculiarly adapted for the task of social organization, aimed chiefly at the principle of exclusion; bringing together a community of people, whose whole life and pursuits, trades, occupations, professions, pleasures, pastimes, were all to be regulated and characterized by one religious impulse. For its accomplishment some of the unexceptionable elements of socialism were needed, in order to cement the whole mass of the congregation and support its economical interests.

I will premise, however, that communism in the form of the Phalanstery was not adopted, and, with the exception of its first application in America, where it lasted about twenty years, it formed no feature of the Brethren's communities. These interests of the individual required a mutual protection, and, on this account, the number of trades was limited, no one having the privilege of pursuing his occupation unless granted him by the authorities of the congregation.

The general proprietary was called the Diacony,

which held the lands, farms, and all the larger establishments under its control and direction, the revenues being applied to the general purposes of the village and the society at large. Under this form of organization competition in trade was effectually excluded, and the community was enabled to flourish by a harmony of industrial pursuits, for, in following out the details of this system, we find that care was taken not to allow one tradesman to under-sell the other; the prices of all goods offered for sale were limited, and the quality of all manufactured articles inspected and kept up to a certain standard. Under these regulations the great principle was implied, that the love of gain was never to enter into the aims of those engaged in trade, but that the desire of benefiting one's neighbor should be the paramount object of an industrious life.

All the necessary rules were laid down for the mutual conduct of master and apprentice, the bearing of each toward the other; fidelity to contract in the making and delivery of goods; as to the circumspect choice of trades for the boys, and a proper discretion in allowing them to follow their inclinations in this particular.

Another institution was the almonry, or poor-fund, with its almoner, who administered to the wants of the destitute, whenever they came to be in need of help, through disease or other causes.

Physicians were regularly appointed by the general superintendence of the village, and paid their stipulated salaries; no fees were ever allowed to be given them; they were required to be married men, to call down Divine assistance in their efforts to cure, and never to boast of their own efficiency in the course of their practice.

It was enjoined upon the physician that he should never forbear disclosing to his patient his real condition, since it was pre-supposed that every one would rejoice, on learning he was approaching nearer to Jesus.

In the Zinzendorfian community egotism became an oblation to a high spiritual purpose; the inner life of its people derived its sustenance from a pure, simple, and active faith, and all their acquisitions were made subservient to spiritual ends. A total surrender of egotism was, accordingly, the first step to membership in this people, fashioned after the old apostolic times. Zinzendorf ushered in his plan by the erection of a house for single Brethren and one for single Sisters. He divided his congregation into "Choirs," or classes: the younger girls, the elder girls, the sisters, the married brethren and sisters, the widows, widowers, the younger boys, the elder boys, the single brethren, all constituted distinct "Choirs," and had their stated and special meetings.

In the institution of the Brethren's and Sisters' Houses, the plan intended was, to afford an asylum to all the young men and women of the community. In Herrnhut we find every young man has his allotted room in the Brethren's House, where he repairs whenever he choses, if not a constant resident of the institution, and pays his tax for its support. The same rule applies to the Sisters' House, in reference to the young women. Many of either sex, who have no means of support under the parental roof, make choice of these abodes, and pursue their employments there. A principal[1] has the superintendence of each of these institutions, and, in the Sisters' House, the inmates of which generally number about two hundred, numerous assistants, or vice-principals, are appointed, who are set over smaller divisions of the sisters.

The aged lady presiding over the Sisters' House at Herrnhut for nearly half a century, was the Countess of Einsiedlen. Her estates and private dwelling were contiguous to the village, but she repaired regularly to the Sisters' House to perform her duties there, and was highly respected and esteemed by those under her charge. She faithfully administered the duties of this office up to the time of her death, which occurred only a few years ago. To explain this circumstance more fully, it may be necessary to state, that the Moravians received a large share of patronage from the nobility, and numbers of titled personages adopted their forms, and became devoted followers of their faith.

The office of this principal and her assistants is to

---

[1] Called Pfleger and Pflegerin, or one who cares for those under him or her.

keep under their constant supervision all the young women residing within the walls of this asylum. All the young girls of the village have their appointments in the building, and assemble there before proceeding to church service, followed by their principals. Over all these female "Choirs" the principal exercises a spiritual influence, guides their conduct, and has confidential communications with them at stated times, such as preceding a communion or Choir Festival.

The institution of the "Speaking," or the confidential communication between the principal and those under her charge, the plan of the Sisters' House itself and its whole organization, have been regarded by many as bearing a strong tinge of Roman Catholicism, and this, with many other features of striking resemblance to the Roman Church, drew upon the Moravians the charge of Romanism, and originated the saying that, "The road to Rome went through Herrnhut."[1] The inmates of these houses,

[1] It is very properly remarked by Lynar: "It appears to me that they who designate the United Brethren as a Lutheran monastic order, labor under a great misconception. There is, confessedly, a certain form of monasticism in their general subordination, obedience to superiors, allotted hours of worship, and other prescribed rules and social forms. But if we reflect how it is marked by its celibacy, its withdrawal from all the usual forms of industry, its seclusion, its mendicancy, the frequent application of coercion in the entrance to the cloister, and the large revenues falling to its use, we shall see the vast difference between the two; and, laying

however, were never bound by promises or vows to remain within their walls, nor did they immure themselves therein for any longer time than the ordinary necessities of life might render it desirable for them to sojourn there. For the most part, they are given to industrious pursuits, they mingle with society, come and go at their pleasure, and when the chance of marriage presents itself, they are at liberty to leave.

The institution of the Brethren's and Sisters' Houses is a marked feature of the Zinzendorfian plan, and tends, perhaps more than any other arrangement, to cement the whole social body residing in a single village. Under this organization there can be but little poverty and no destitution, for while all the members of the religious family, as it may justly be viewed, are cared for, helplessness and old age are the objects of a peculiar tenderness and sympathy. Another characteristic of Herrnhut was, the consecration of manual labor, and its elevation to the position of a religious duty.

As the aims of the whole people were concentrated upon one purpose, that of first seeking their own chasteness of life, and thence setting out upon the apostolic mission among mankind, labor enjoyed its dignity, and the trades, occupations, and professions

---

aside all other considerations, we cannot but acknowledge that one has proved as great a benefit to the State as the other has been prejudicial."

of all were sanctified, and received the benedictions of prayer and song.

Much stress should be laid upon this aspect of Moravian life, inasmuch as it serves to show how the asperities of toil for daily bread were mitigated, how the contrasts of society were subdued, and the condition of those gifted with fortune and those born without estate fully equalized; for, notwithstanding the equality aimed at by Zinzendorf, both of these grades of society have existed at all times in every Moravian community, and in Europe, where the distinction between noble and peasant is so strongly and indelibly marked, the Christianity acted, and does yet act, with a subduing influence.

At Herrnhut, the Diacony or Proprietary of the farms, wood lands, hotel, stores, and large manufactories is still upheld, and is based upon the fundamental principle of Zinzendorf's plan, to perpetuate the congregation by a blending of interests, and making the whole membership intent upon one purpose.

The Diacony is sustained in all the European communities, although recently abolished in this country, and is connected with a lease system, giving the right of holding real estate to those only who are members of a congregation. Thus by excluding all foreign elements from the population of a small village communion, the tone of society can be upheld in comparative purity; all the forms of the church, its rituals, festivals, and enjoinments preserved, and the Christian family, after the early apostolic model, and in accordance with the idea of Zinzendorf, fully carried out. Hence the village, and it only, became the seat of a fully-developed Moravianism; because its perfect isolation, its uniformity, its conjoint purposes and pursuits, and its unique cultus removed it beyond, and elevated it above, the atmosphere of a grosser world; all these rendered it the true sphere of an apostolic Christianity, and fulfilled the ideal of a perfect congregation.[1]

---

[1] The admission into the community of Herrnhut was not a matter of easy accomplishment, and before permission was granted to any one to become a member of the society, he was required to hand into the ecclesiastical board a written declaration of his intentions.

The Board, or Conference, then requested of him a personal interview, in which a candid declaration of his sentiments was asked. He was told that the congregation was looked upon as a wise institution of Christ, which was partly destined to spread His kingdom among infidels and heathen, and partly for the fulfillment of the testament of Jesus, which enjoins unity and a close connection among his believers as the only condition of happiness, and the sole means of protection against the tide of worldly vanity, that involves so many in ruin.

It was not presumed that an individual was more sure of his salvation within than without the congregation, if he only belonged to the true church of Christ, which is invisible, and consists of such members as really believe in Jesus Christ, and give practical evidence of this belief.

It was, therefore, not sufficient to be a Christian to gain admittance to the congregation, but a proper appreciation, and a peculiar endowment were deemed requisite.

God was not willing that all true Christians should join

To render more united this community of thought and labor, Zinzendorf applied to Moravian worship

---

this congregation, since he wishes them to be scattered throughout the earth as useful seed; on this account it could enjoy its friendships beyond its own circle, without proselyting.

The initiation to the congregation was a matter of deep moment, and demanded much wary reflection, because every one who assumed its responsibilities must pledge his life for Christ, be prepared for every summons, and live after the manner of the Apostles, when it was said of them, "they devoted themselves to the Lord," and consequently to the congregation.

The candidate was at liberty to reside several weeks among the Brethren, and make himself fully acquainted with them, before closing his purpose to join them.

During this period he was questioned as to his past career—what had been his fortunes in the world; was he out at service or at home with his parents; or were there any obstacles in the way, rendering it impracticable for him to come among them. The main question put to him was, how he had come to think of seeking his salvation, and what had led him to apply to them. It was never inquired whether he were rich, or poor, or what were his abilities.

After all scruples and objections had been surmounted, and the applicant remained firm in his purpose and conviction that he considered himself called to become a member of the Herrnhutian community, the lot was resorted to; should this result in the negative, he was told he could not be accepted; if, on the contrary, in the affirmative, he was received.

He now had permission to stay, and was regarded as a candidate for admission. He visited the Brother, who is the adviser or principal of the Choir to which he was destined, and conversed with him in the most confidential manner.

It was now considered by the Conference of Elders, whether

all the embellishments of music, the festival, the uniformity of head-dress among the sisters, the

---

the lot should be used for his final entrance into the communion of the society, and if it proved a negative he was apprised of it, and no further action was taken in his case until it was thought that time had removed the hindrance. If now the lot approved of him, it was announced to the whole assembled congregation that Brother —— would be received as a member on the following Congregation-Day, which occurred every month.

The reception of the new Brother took place in the evening of this day, after the usual discourse was ended.

The candidate sat before the minister, who impressed upon him the duties and obligations connected with the step he had taken, and held out to him the share of spiritual blessings dispensed by Jesus, which he would receive; promising him, at the same time, the reciprocal duties the congregation owed him.

Then all arose, and during the singing of a liturgy, the new candidate was received with the kiss of peace, bestowed, according to the sex, by Elder or Eldress.

The minister, finally, with the whole assembly, knelt down and prayed, and the ordinance was concluded with singing.

This was the entrance into the Congregation; the next step was to become a candidate for the Holy Communion.

This also became a subject for the Elders' Conference, who appealed to the lot to know if the time was come for his partaking of this sacred rite. When an affirmative was given, he was notified through his Choir adviser to attend the Communion Love-Feast, as a spectator.

Here it was made known that he was about to become a candidate for the Sacrament. When it was thought the proper time had arrived, the Conference once more resorted to the lot, to know if he was prepared for admission, and if the reply was favorable, he was desired to be in readiness at the next white dress on select occasions, and numerous other regulations, intended to imbue with order the whole structure he had erected.[1]

If a reflection of Roman Catholicism has been here and there recognized in the drama of the worship of Herrnhut, we shall find its church architecture the farthest possible departure from it. The poverty of its early pioneers, and the necessity of expending its surplus funds in the work of the missions, rendered superfluous all ornaments of the sanctuary. The church at Herrnhut presents no pulpit, no cushioned seats, no columns, no festooned drapery; nothing but a simple table raised upon a dais, for the performance of all religious exercises. Although now its ample means would enable it to erect an edifice in modern style, with all the accessories of fashionable worship, yet the adherence to

---

ceremonial. A few hours before the Communion, his adviser summoned him, and, in presence of the Pastor and several other members, prayed over him, sung verses, and, during the singing, washed his feet. When the newly-received member was a Sister, this was done by the female Principal, in presence of the Eldresses. (See Lynar.)

[1] In paying this tribute to the Count's memory, we must ascribe to him the remodeling, rather than the original construction, of the new Moravian Church. The old Moravian and Bohemian emigrants to Herrnhut, who formed the material for this new organization of 1722, were extremely tenacious of their old forms, rituals and hymns, and out of those elements Herrnhut, organized under the auspices of Zinzendorf, sprung up.

the old in thought, form, and general modes of life is so deeply rooted, that it stands there in all its simplicity, untouched.

One of the few customs of the early days of Herrnhut that have now become extinct, was that of the Night-watch. This office was instituted in 1727, when the village was but small, the people in their first love, and a greater zeal felt for this kind of nocturnal guard than would be the case at the present time. In the winter evenings, the watchman commenced his rounds at eight o'clock, and continued until six in the morning. In summer, he began at nine o'clock, and closed his duties at four o'clock. This office was assumed by all the male inhabitants in rotation, from sixteen to sixty years.

The announcement of the hour in verse rendered the custom peculiarly beautiful; thus at eight o'clock was sung:—

The clock is eight! to Herrnhut all is told
How Noah and his Seven were saved of old.

9 o'clock. Hear, Brethren, hear! the hour of nine is come;
Keep pure each heart and chasten every home.

10 o'clock. Hear, Brethren, hear! now ten the hour-hand shows;
They only rest, who long for night's repose.

11 o'clock. The clock's eleven! and ye have heard it all
How in that hour the mighty God did call.

12 o'clock. It's midnight now! and at that hour ye know
With lamps to meet the bridegroom we must go.

1 o'clock. The hour is one! through darkness steals the day;
Shines in your hearts the morning star's first ray?

2 o'clock. The clock is two! who comes to meet the day,
And to the Lord of days his homage pay?
3 o'clock. The clock is three! the Three in One above
Let body, soul and spirit truly love.
4 o'clock. The clock is four! where'er on earth are three,
The Lord has promised He the fourth will be.
5 o'clock. The clock is five! while five away were sent,
Five other virgins to the marriage went.
6 o'clock. The clock is six! and from the watch I'm free,
And every one may his own watchman be.[1]

But this sentinel of Zion was not confined to the set stanzas; he continued his edifying verses during his entire rounds. In singing these hymns he frequently awoke the sleepers, who found the subject suited to their own situations, and the impressions of the night caused by those appropriate songs often had their enduring effect. It is related that during the visit of a certain nobleman to Herrnhut, he was so delighted with this primitive custom that he insisted upon assuming the watch for an entire night, and went the rounds in the usual form.

During the same epoch of Moravian fervor the institution of the "Hourly Prayer" took its rise. A company of twenty-four brethren and as many sisters (afterwards increased to seventy-two) came together and pledged themselves to occupy one hour in the twenty-four, each in his or her turn, and employ it in intercession for himself or herself and others, wherever known and in need of aid from

[1] Composed by Zinzendorf.

above. The hour thus allotted to each one was drawn by lot, and at whatever time of day or night it might fall, they were to be found at their posts, devoted to the charge assigned them.

The Night-watch and Hourly Prayer were somewhat similar in tendency. Neither aimed at a protection from without, but the design was rather to guard the life within, and it formed another of those essential points in a perfect Christian organization, complete in all its parts, which distinguished the system of the Moravians above all similar religious communities on record.

Previous to the settlement of Herrnhut, Count Zinzendorf spent his early youth with his grandmother, who lived on her estates at Great Hennersdorf, at the distance of three miles from the village. The old Castle of Hennersdorf, distinctly seen from Herrnhut, is an interesting object of research to the visitor. Leaving the highway, and entering an avenue of lindens, you are conducted beneath their shade up to the very entrance of the former courtyard of the castle, now converted to the purposes of a barn-yard; and on inquiring for the forest-keeper, who resides in its lower rooms, which are heavy-looking, massive, vaulted chambers, he receives you with a welcome, reaches for the key, and guides you up through its dilapidated corridors and empty halls, where there is a cold dreary feeling reigning throughout. The tapestry of a former century hangs upon the walls in tattered fragments; and in looking out through its windows upon the pleasant domains around, you are reminded of the past history connected with the venerable pile, over which many centuries have already passed. The forest-keeper himself, the official to whom I have already alluded, resides here, and has the care of the woods of the Unity, or General Proprietary. He seems to take an interest in the history and traditions of the old castle, and gives many particulars in regard to its earlier annals, but leaves some films of doubt resting upon them, as to his verity as a chronicler.

Near to the Castle of Hennersdorf stands a venerable church, under the care of its aged Lutheran pastor, who, having the keys of its vaults, leads the inquisitive stranger thither to exhibit the remains of the widow von Gersdorf, the Count's grandmother, which are still perfect and uninjured by time.

In sketching the characteristics of Herrnhut, as they have been and still are, I find much that is essential in Moravianism to be derived from the national character and the language of the people who gave it birth. A century has effected but little change in the modes of life, or in the expressions of feeling of a people, who, in common with those of Southern and Middle Europe, are children of emotion. Born and trained up in abstemiousness, the early German Moravians were better fitted for endurance and privation, such as fell to their lot in the missionary field, than any other race of people; but through all the vicissitudes of want and suffering, the language of their infancy, the social customs of their forefathers, the hymns of Zinzendorf, Paul Gerhard, Luise von Hayn and others shielded and solaced them.

In the language and heart of the German people we discover a key to much that would otherwise be inexplicable in the phraseology of the early Moravian Brethren. Its forms of worship approach so nearly to nature, are so divested of art, if we except the application of the sound classic music which adorns it, that we cannot account for its derivation but by looking into German social life. Here we find the emotions declared in language. Sentimentality becomes a living truth, and is acted as we find it written in our poetry. The colloquial scenes of the family might be copied, and they would appear like fiction. Upon this characteristic of German emotional thought was founded that essential portion of the Zinzendorfian theology which relates to the Saviour. In the old Hennersdorf Castle, the window is still shown where he is said to have thrown out letters to the Saviour, when a child, and it is remarkable that the child remained a portion of his character to the last. From the very commencement of his early experience, Christ's personality seized upon his heart and mind, and his imaginary intercourse, which he felt to be real, was with a being whom he knew to be a brother. To give vent to the impressions springing out of that intercourse, he indulged in expressions and composed lyrical strains, in which the language and the social element of the race of that country exhibited their strongest infusion. Much of the censure attached to Zinzendorf's phraseology among the English and Americans, arose from the simple fact of their not taking this view of German life. What appears so artificial and theatrical to us, is perfectly natural to the German people, and this explanation renders clear and explicable, what sometimes appears to be the puerility of Moravianism.

In the church of Herrnhut, and in the old edifice of Berthelsdorf, the gathering for worship is marked by the most respectful decorum. In these monarchical countries, subordination and respect for authority are striking features, and it is pleasing to observe the quiet and passiveness of life among those who esteem it a religious duty to submit to the endless rules of conventionality, order, and law, that distinguish the society of Central Europe.

Upon certain days of the year there is an assembling of the "Diaspora"[1] Brethren at Herrnhut, or of such members of the church as are scattered

---

[1] The "Diaspora," or dispersed congregation, dates as far back as 1742, when it was found necessary to establish a traveling ministry, to enable all such as desired the intercourse of the Brethren, to come within their influence and enjoy their teachings. This division of the society is confined to Germany and the continent, where it includes all classes, and is now so far extended as to number 40,000 members in Livonia, and not less than 100,000 in Germany, Switzerland, and the south of France.

throughout the surrounding country, but are not united together in a congregation. On these occasions the audience is a very large one, the church being of ample size, and it is an interesting moment when this devout crowd is seen coming and going. Among this widely-spread "Diaspora" are found many exemplary specimens of the Brethren; and whether on the estate, with its mansion, or in the lowly cot and its few acres, the excellence of Christianity shines forth.

In common with the usages and naïve etiquette of German life, seen everywhere, the social forms of the family at Herrnhut are expressive of its general religious system. Before sitting down, and after rising from meals, the host and hostess give you their hands, and wish you *Ein gesegnete mahlzeit!*[1] and *Ich wünsche wohl gespeist zu haben!*[2] Then, if in summer, a stroll in the garden follows, or an hour in the "Laube," until the time for coffee has approached, when a fragrant cup of this beverage is enjoyed, some regaling cigars, pleasant reading, and abundance of conversation. The birth-day is an event of no little importance, and the entertainment of friends, who come in large numbers to pay their congratulations, is a matter conscientiously observed.

---

[1] A blessed meal!

[2] I hope you have dined well! As this ceremony generally accompanies the dinner, the first salutation precedes, and the second follows the meal.

If we regard these old institutions, these poetical customs, the pure Zinzendorfian Moravianism, with all its unique, simple rituals, still exhibited at Herrnhut, we must conclude that time there effects no changes as it does among us. Its people do not seem intent upon building up a new future every day, but, looking back upon the past, they dwell there in thought and cling to its observance with tenacious grasp.

These are some of the characteristics of Herrnhut as it now is, and I have forborne to dilate upon many points brought into notice, since they serve but as a text for the delineations of Moravian life in America, such as it has been. In describing the organization of the village congregation here among ourselves, we shall behold the counterpart of living Herrnhut, which we are to regard as the original and the model.[1]

---

[1] A distinguished testimony has been given to Herrnhut, its system, and the character of its founder, by Dr. Loo, Professor in Halle, who thus writes :—

"At a time when such a general dispersion took place, Zinzendorf gathered together. Herrnhut may be said to have realized the full accomplishment for church and social life what our times are in quest of: a moral order in human relations, a union of the evangelical confessions, an emancipation of church from state, and following out her true designs, both as regards internal relations as well as the position she naturally stands in toward the State. Herrnhut, certainly, is not to be pointed out as a complete model for practical purposes, but, regarded as an instrument of instruction, it teaches us all we need. Its organization was adapted for a certain length of time to the preservation, propagation, and discharge of the great work of humanity, and this was to be done in limited circles, but *here* and in *full.*

"As theological science began to undermine the temple of the Lord, Zinzendorf, aided chiefly by poor and simple people, and ridiculed by the learned and educated, succeeded in bearing away the altar and its sanctuary, and even with these the veil which he might at one time extend before him, into a tent that stood upon a firm foundation, in order to save them for the whole world of Protestantism.

"This is a part of the world's history, the merit of which belongs to him, and far surpasses that of all the philosophers from his time up to our own, who are driven like waves, one against the other, until they reach the firmly built shore of revelation.

"Zinzendorf himself regarded his institution only as a transition; he made the declaration that whenever the gospel should burst forth in a more luminous appearance than was exhibited among the Brethren, they should unite themselves with the new dispensation, and that they were in a manner pledged to do so. The mannerism of Zinzendorf, with his unique and singular forms of expression, (though many of his intrinsic beauties have passed unregarded,) has been made the subject of frequent rebuke. But this very characteristic has preserved his people from communication with the mongrel and the impure; from the contagion of the worst grade of moral leprosy that could possibly come in contact with a work like his; and to which it must inevitably fall a prey as soon as it puts on these attractive forms, which all the world admires."

IV.

ZINZENDORF.

"He believed because he loved."

In estimating individual greatness, we generally place before the mind some standard of merit by which to weigh the performances of him who excites our wonder and admiration.

The world has many standards to which its ideas of greatness must necessarily conform, and those are often so falsely laid down that society is misled by the factitious glare that accumulates around men of note. In some men, to all appearances, the heart has no room for action, so that to the end of their lives it leaves no memories of its sensitive loves, its diffusive tenderness, or the pleasant influences by which it binds man to man. In others, on the contrary, the history of emotion is an expansive representation of an individual career, and when eminence springs from this source it shows how a heroism may originate within the inner workings of a pure and chastened mind.

The value and importance of such a history as that of the heart under the finest religious influences, are nowhere more striking than in the personage known as Count Zinzendorf. If ancient descent and long-worn titles were of any value, his position, as a nobleman, was of great eminence, while his claims to distinction on the score of inherited rank were by no means small, for the illustrious family from which he sprung traced an ancestry as far back as the eleventh century, at which period it was ranked among the twelve great houses, which were considered the chief support of the Austrian dynasty. He was entitled Nicholas Lewis, Count and Lord of Zinzendorf and Pottendorf; Lord of the Baronies of Freydeck, Schoeneck, Thürnstein, and the Vale of Wachovia; Lord of the Manor of Upper, Lower, and Middle Berthelsdorf; Hereditary Warder of the Chase to His Imperial Majesty, in the Duchy of Austria, etc. etc. He was born in the City of Dresden on the 26th of May, 1700, and on the same day was baptized in the presence of several sponsors, among whom was Dr. Spener. His father died within a few months after his birth; and, just before his death, his infant son was brought to him to receive his blessing, but the expiring parent exclaimed when he beheld him:—"My dear son, I am expected to give you my blessing, but you are already happier than I, although I am nearly at the throne of Christ!"

In 1704 his mother married a second time, when the youth was placed under the care of his grandmother, the widow Henriette, of Gersdorf, who lived at Groshennersdorf. She was a lady of distinguished piety and acquirements, which were even of a classical order, as we are told of her having conducted considerable epistolary correspondence in the Latin language, and was in constant communication with Franke, Spener, Anton, Von Canstein, and other men of their class. She was, at the same time, a poetess, and, like many of her cotemporaries, possessed the ready gift of rendering her Christian feelings in German verse. Happily the young nobleman, until his tenth year, remained under the protection of this superior woman, and during the course of these innocent days at Groshennersdorf, many little incidents are related, which illustrate the quality of his mind, and point to the leading aim and direction of his future character.

It is said that when the army of Charles XII. of Sweden penetrated into Saxony, some of his soldiers intruded upon the privacy of Hennersdorf Castle just at the moment when the young Zinzendorf was engaged at his wonted employment of holding communion with his Saviour in the attitude of fervent prayer, and that they were so struck with the scene before them, a child of only six years of age exhibiting such earnest devotion, and so sanctified a demeanor, that their purposes were disarmed, and they joined in with his devotional exercises.

After this he was removed to the Royal School at Halle, under the superintendence of Franke, where he was regarded as a youth of great abilities, and made rapid progress in learning. He could compose a Greek oration at sixteen, and speak extemporaneously in Latin on a given subject. But Zinzendorf's heart ever kept pace with his intellect; and during his six years stay at the University of Halle, the friendship of the venerable Franke fostered his early inclinations, already nurtured and encouraged by his grandmother, and the association with his school companions gave rise to the institution among a select number of them, known as the "Senfkorn Orden," or the "Order of the Mustard Seed." The statutes of this order are still extant, and their purport is, "to follow Christ in walk and conversation, to love your neighbor, and strive for the conversion of Jews and heathen." The badge was a shield, bearing upon it the representation of an "*Ecce Homo*," with the words inscribed on it, "*His wounds our healing.*" Baron Frederick de Watteville was among the members of the union, and he, together with many others of its chosen number, became a devoted follower of the cause it represented.

Growing apace in Christian love, and adorned with the accomplishments of mind which he received at Halle, the Count was now sent to the University of Wittenberg to learn jurisprudence. It was customary for persons of his rank to go through the incidental practices of fencing, riding, and dancing, studies that were little in accordance with his tastes, and while undergoing their initiation, he prayed that the Lord might quicken his capacity for them, to enable him the sooner to pass through them. His poetical inclination evinced itself at the age of twelve years, from which time, throughout the years devoted to his education, he wrote verses, expressive of the same sentiment found throughout the memoirs of his whole inner life. His course at Wittenberg lasted three years, and during this time he devoted a large part of his attention to theological pursuits, and the disputations in which the theologians of Halle and Wittenberg were at issue; and having closed his career there, he was placed under the tutelage of a new preceptor, and commenced his travels.

He went to Holland, and, on his way thither, passing through Dusseldorf, saw among the paintings of that school an *Ecce Homo*, with this inscription, "I have done this for thee, what wilt thou do for me?" It made a singular impression upon him, and was the subject of immediate prayer.

From Holland he proceeded to Paris, and here, having been introduced into gay society, he found himself surrounded with all its fascinations. In addition to the prestige of rank, Zinzendorf's person and lineament of countenance, with its mild benignity, must have rendered all the higher circles accessible to him, and we find in the account given of his Parisian life, that he was everywhere a welcome and a courted guest. His friendships here were not only cultivated among the secular classes, but he found himself mingled with the Catholic clergy, and, of those, one of his most intimate associates was the Cardinal de Noailles. The Catholics used strong persuasions to draw him over to themselves, and long discussions ensued between the young Count and the Cardinal, without, however, alluring him from preconceived ideas, or his own forms of uttering Christ's love and sacrifice, which he found more congenial than those in the sensuous glare of the Roman worship, as presented to his mind and imagination.

He soon left Paris and its seductive influences, and, returning to Saxony by way of Bavaria, he went through Castell, where he visited his aunt, the Countess of Castell. This visit was marked by one of those passages in opening manhood, where the early affections come into play, and in which Zinzendorf exhibited himself in all his fullness. The opening of this scene in the young Count's life was an acquaintance with his cousin, Theodora, daughter of the widow of Castell. The casual acquaintance ripened into an affection, which, from the details of that episode in the biography handed down to us by his friend, Spangenberg, in which the confessions are artlessly given by the Countess herself, forty years afterwards, appears to have been more strongly developed on his part than on her own. The aged Countess relates how, at the time of her first intimacy with her youthful and ardent cousin, she received him in the most cordial and affectionate manner, giving him her miniature at his departure, and expressing the wish of a speedy renewal of his visit.

This he misunderstood as a tacit acquiescence in the proposals he had indirectly made, under the smiles of the mother of Theodora. The young lady herself, however, experienced no feelings other than those of a kinswoman's ordinary affection, and was afterwards deeply grieved that she had given her young cousin cause for hope. They parted from each other in this state of feeling, and Zinzendorf happening to visit Count Henry Reuss, in Ebersdorf, learned, in the course of familiar conversation, that the latter was about choosing a wife, that his mother had set her heart upon Theodora of Castell, as a suitable consort for him, but that she had waived this choice altogether, knowing that Zinzendorf had made the first claim in that direction. He now showed the strong bent of his character, put his faith in practice, regarded the event as the Divine finger pointing to him some other destiny as his connubial allotment, and voluntarily offered to sacrifice to his friend all his preconceived affections for the lady, who thence became the wife of Count Reuss, and whose nuptials were celebrated by Zinzendorf himself in prayers and hymns.

On his return to Dresden, his rank entitled him to certain civil offices under government, but he felt such an extreme repugnance to all secular employment that it was long before he could be prevailed on to accept a seat in the public councils, under the title of Aulic and Justicial Counsellor; but at the very moment he was assuming this official dignity in the State, he resolved to make the preaching of the gospel the destiny of his future life.

Having then engaged some assistants in the work, he commenced a system of religious instruction, and held regular devotional meetings. He was so fully absorbed in this one purpose, that everything else was made subservient to it, and when he found that the claims of rank became a restraint upon the obligations of an apostle of Christ, he felt anxious to set aside his worldly titles, and sink to the level of an ordinary citizen.

In 1732 he was married to the Countess Erdmuth Dorothea von Reuss, sister of Henry von Reuss, to whom allusion has just been made in the incidents of Castell. This noble lady possessed qualities of mind and heart of the highest order, making her deserving of the most conspicuous place in the biography of Moravian women. She was well fitted for the work she was entering upon, as the wife of Zinzendorf, and the circumstances of their marriage were unusual and unprecedented in the history of all similar contracts. After transferring to her all his property, he entered into a covenant with his youthful partner, that they should both be ready, at a moment's warning from the Lord, to enter upon the mission, take up the pilgrim's staff, and ever be prepared to endure the scoffs of mankind. How implicitly they mutually fulfilled this heavenly pledge is seen in the sequel of their lives.

Previous to his marriage the Count had entered

upon his duties as proprietor of the manor and estates of Berthelsdorf, on which occasion he was proclaimed lord of the manor, and received the usual tributes of respect and homage from the vassals occupying them. These, as before described, lay in Upper Lusatia, and had been purchased by Zinzendorf, after selling his hereditary property, out of a large portion of which he had been defrauded through the unfaithfulness of a steward.

Soon after this event, the arrival of Christian David and his fellow-pilgrims, exiles from Moravia, and the descendants of the Ancient Unitas Fratrum, took place. Christian David himself was a remarkable man, and somewhat after the Count's own heart. He was first introduced to the notice of the latter by his steward, and permission was given him and his company to take refuge at Berthelsdorf.

When Zinzendorf performed his wedding-tour he found himself entering, during the darkness of night, upon his own domain, and beheld at some distance through the trees a small light; on a nearer approach, he discovered it to be the newly-erected habitation of the Moravian emigrants; he descended from his carriage, entered the door, and joined the little band in fervent prayer and hymns.

The sudden growth of the small society, now springing up around the Hutberg, to which the name of Herrnhut was given, the warm spirit and somewhat enthusiastic disposition of the Count and his people, excited the wonder and admiration of the country around. With this, however, slander, misrepresentation, and ill-feeling were combined, leading to a steady contest from within a few years after the foundation of Herrnhut until the year 1736, when the government of Saxony deemed it necessary to probe the truth of the complaints promulgated against the Brethren. The storm that was now about to visit Herrnhut had first gathered around the head of its founder himself; under the pretext of his disseminating false doctrines, his enemy, Count Brühl, succeeded in obtaining a decree from the Saxon government, banishing him from its territory. This event, which occurred in March, 1736, was soon after followed by a royal commission sent to investigate the Herrnhutian community, its usages, social forms, and practices. The commission was favorably received, and the results of the examination proving satisfactory, no immediate steps were taken to disturb Herrnhut and its people.

On hearing of his banishment, Count Wächtersbach gave Zindendorf an invitation to occupy the Ronneberg, whither he accordingly repaired, accompanied by his family, Christian David, De Watteville and others, who formed his retinue, and called themselves the Pilgrim Congregation. But before they proceeded to the Ronneberg, Christian David had been sent to explore the proposed quarters destined for the temporary sojourn of the exiles, and his report to the Count was made in words as little flattering as could well be conceived. The habitation was so forbidding that he advised him not to go there. "Have you not been in Greenland, Christian?" asked the Count. "Yes," replied he; "if it were but Greenland."

The old pile stands to this day upon the summit of a craggy eminence, commanding a view of the town of Hanau, and of the road over which Napoleon passed, on his return from the battle of Leipsic. It is an ancient ruin, having been founded at some distant point of time, when knight, baron, lance and buckler were familiar terms, and held their sway over these domains. When the Count and his friends moved into it, they found the denizens of the gray old castle a motley set of Jews, Separatists, and people of every strange creed, who lived there in the capacity of peddlers, mendicants, and mechanics, and sheltered themselves in its dusky recesses and vacant halls.

When Zinzendorf and his suite made their first entrance into this singular abode, the inhabitants of the place presented to the newly arrived pilgrims a most repulsive and cheerless appearance, and we may readily fancy the character of the scene presented at the moment when they landed at the threshold of that old feudal structure. In spite, however, of all discouragements, the Ronneberg became and remained the dwelling-place of the Pilgrim Congregation, and it was here the Count entered upon his first term of banishment. The chief employment of himself and followers was to teach the children loitering around the premises they occupied; then a small congregation was formed, out of which the larger communities of the Wetterau grew up in succeeding years, known as Marienborn and Herrnhaag. This portion of Germany was favorable to the rise and progress of an early, imaginative, and over-excited Moravianism, having been the field of the activity of Spener, whose influence was strongly felt in the formation of these congregations.

Duly settled at the Ronneberg, and having arranged the affairs of his congregation, which was greatly augmenting, the Count commenced traveling from place to place, enlarging the sphere of his labors. At this time he was wont to travel by whatever mode he found most convenient—frequently by the public coach, often on foot; and, in his interviews with persons with whom he delighted to associate, he sometimes conversed for ten hours in succession. In these journeyings, he would frequently set out in the afternoon and pursue his rambles till midnight, often with an empty purse.

One of the characteristic incidents of this period was his interview with the King of Prussia. During his stay at Berlin, Frederick William I. desired to see him, and, through his chaplain, Jablonsky, appointed the place of conference at the royal hunting lodge of Wusterhausen. He questioned the Count as to all the various points of doctrine he held, and upon finding, from the nature of his replies, that they were pure and unimpeachable, he declared he had been deceived by the numerous false reports he had heard, and became his sincere friend, corresponding with him until his death, in 1740. It was one year after the interview that the king himself, requested Jablonsky to confer the episcopal ordination upon him, which took place at his subsequent visit to Berlin, in 1737.

During the year 1736 he is seen in England, seeking the friendship of the venerable Archbishop of Canterbury, John Potter. This dignitary disclosed the most liberal sentiments toward the Count and the Brethren, acknowledging their claims to an uninterrupted line of bishops, since the days of the Waldenses, and charging them to preserve the jewel that had thus fallen to their inheritance. He remarked, at the same time, to Bishop Nitschmann, that no Englishman, versed in ecclesiastical history, could deny the episcopal succession of the Brethren, a point on the authenticity of which they have always laid great stress, as strengthening the claims of their little Bohemian and Moravian church to the purity of its origin.

In the year 1737, being fifteen months after his departure from Herrnhut, he was once more recalled to Saxony, and permission was given him to remain under certain conditions. The Count was happy to find himself again at Herrnhut, the first seat of his early spiritual love; met his congregation, and sung, in the fervor of the moment, one of his frequent improvisations,—

> "Zufriedene Gemeine,
> In Jesu Blute reine."

But his conscience would not allow him to sign the act of his recall, and he thenceforth became a voluntary exile for the ten succeeding years. The early portion of the ensuing year was spent in Berlin, where he preached to multitudes of people of all classes and conditions; and his discourses held in this city are among his most esteemed productions. They were taken down by John De Watteville, afterwards his son-in-law, and preserved among his writings.

In the year 1739, we find Zinzendorf in the Island of St. Thomas, where the efforts of the Moravian Brethren were not a little frustrated by the combined opposition they met with from the authorities of the island. The negroes themselves readily accepted the ministrations of the missionaries, and the Count found himself in the midst of a congregation of seven hundred souls. In two days after his arrival, he made himself conversant with the Creole language, and preached to and wrote for the negroes in their own tongue. Leaving St. Thomas with a parting address in his usual pathetic vein, he returned by way of the islands of St. John and St. Croix, visiting the graves of those martyrs who had already fallen in the service of the Lord, victims to the West Indian climate. During his stay in St.

Eustatia, he found time to compose one of his most admired hymns,—

> "The Saviour's blood and righteousness
> My beauty is, my glorious dress."

In an extremely shattered state of health, the consequence of the voyage to the West Indies, he returned to Marienborn, in the Wetterau, whence, after being reinstated in health, he again set out on his travels through Germany and Switzerland, preaching in almost every place through which he passed. In traversing the Black Forest, he saw the Cloister of St. George, and his fancy suggested that here a Moravian station might be established. The idea was never realized; but it is worthy of note, in connection with this incident, that in 1809 the town of Königsfeld[1] was built on the same eminence, at only three miles distance from that cloister.

In the winter of 1741, we once more find the Count crossing the sea, and landing at New York, accompanied by his daughter Benigna, Anna Nitschmann and others, on his way to the infant colony which had gathered together at Bethlehem, and had taken refuge in the small log dwelling on the banks of the Lehigh. His mission to America, at this time, was one of extreme hazard, as Pennsylvania,

---

[1] Described in an interesting work that has just appeared, entitled "An English Girl's Account of a Moravian Settlement in the Black Forest." London, 1857.

the scene of his labors, in those parts whither his mission directed him, was mostly inhabited by Indians.

Having joined in the celebration of Christmas Eve at Bethlehem, the Count set out in the following year, 1742, on his three Indian journeys, with no other companions than his daughter Benigna, Anna Nitschmann, two other sisters, and eleven brethren, some of whom spoke English and Dutch, together with Conrad Weiser, the colonial interpreter. These Indian excursions were full of adventure. The shelter for the night was usually under pitched tents; the company forded streams with their horses, climbed up pathless hills, and suffered all the discomforts of a rude and savage country. The first of these three Christian embassies to the Indians was to Meniolagomekah, the settlement of the Delawares, but before proceeding thither they paid a visit to the Indian Patemi, who lived near Nazareth, spoke English well, and made them acquainted with the rites, ceremonies and customs of his nation.

His second journey was to Shekomeko, where the Mohicans dwelt, on the boundaries of New York and Connecticut, among whom he baptized six converts. His sojourn under the tent of bark, provided for him by the missionary Rauch, in the depth of a primeval forest, was to him one of unusual enjoyment, and he described the days and nights spent amid these associations as the most pleasant of his life. This was the first Indian congregation, and consisted of ten persons.

In the autumn of the same year, he undertook his third and last journey among the Shawanese, and rapaired to their principal village Wajomick (Wyoming) on the Susquehanna. He was accompanied by two converted Indians, Conrad Weiser, and a few other friends. It was the most perilous of his Indian adventures. The Shawanese themselves were a treacherous tribe, and, during the absence of Weiser, imbibing some suspicions against the Count and his party, they laid a scheme to murder them all. It providentially happened that Weiser had a foreboding of some coming evil, and hurried back barely in time to arrest the intended massacre.

It was on the same occasion that the remarkable preservation of the Count took place, when, on awaking in his tent he found a snake coiled around his neck, which he removed with his own hands. In those rude times churches were scarce; the sanctuary was sought in barns and private houses, and we find Zinzendorf holding forth the doctrines of Herrnhut and singing the hymns of his own lyre within such precincts. He was surrounded and listened to by people of all creeds, as a more heterogeneous mixture of religions than was then to be found in Pennsylvania existed nowhere.

On his appearance in Philadelphia, his demeanor, phraseology, and purposes were but ill understood, and great misconstruction was placed upon them.

In transplanting Herrnhut and Marienborn to a land of such incongruous elements, in transferring the language and thoughts that there found utterance to a new people, living amid different associations and feelings from those of Lusatia, much obloquy and ridicule were brought upon the newly-arrived Moravian emigrants. The hymns of Zinzendorf, as well as the Moravian's general mode of expression, clothed in a literal translation, could scarcely be comprehended, and, where a natural indifference to religious sentiment existed, as was usual among those who showed the greatest coldness and opposition to him, he could attract no sympathy nor receive any appreciation.

The closing scene of his labors in this country was witnessed in the newly-built Moravian Church in Philadelphia, where, on the 31st December, 1742, before a crowded assembly, he preached on the text of the day, Mark xiv. 8: "She hath done what she could," etc. In this discourse he gave a narrative of his performances during his brief stay in America, his preachings, his work among the Indians, and the establishment of numerous congregations throughout the province. At the conclusion of his address, he retired unnoticed by the audience, in order to avoid a formal leave-taking, and drove off in a coach, in waiting for him, to New York, to embark for Europe.

Before his departure, he called on Capt. Garrison, whom he had known in St. Thomas, and who had retired from service, and entreated him to convey him on board his vessel home to Europe. The aged seaman was loath to encounter the dangers of the sea, and declined undertaking another voyage. Zinzendorf told him the vessel this time would ride safely through the stormy ocean; that knowing it, he could predict it; he persisted in his request, and finally succeeded in surmounting the scruples and fears of the aged Garrison, who once more assumed the helm. The voyage lasted six weeks, and was not without its perils, for, when near the Scilly Isles, a violent storm overtook them, and all on board, except Zinzendorf, gave themselves up for lost. Calm and collected, he encouraged the captain to dismiss his fears, for that in two hours the storm would abate. The prediction was verified, for in that time the winds veered to another quarter, and the danger was over. Looking upon his prophecy in the light of a miracle, Garrison asked him how he came to know all this. The Count replied that for twenty years he had been in constant intercourse with his Saviour, that he conferred with Him, and He gave him to know, on this occasion, that the storm would cease in two hours.

The scene of his exertions now were England and the Wetterau, where we find him engaged in the work of building up the church which he had been instrumental in renewing in 1722, and which was taking root in various portions of England, America, Holland, and Germany. The ten years of his exile expired in 1747, and, according to his prediction, he once more obtained leave of the Saxon government to return to Herrnhut, which he found growing in size and improving in the enjoyment of temporal and spiritual blessings.

After the Count's return from America, a serious convulsion commenced with the inner life of the Brethren, which assumed a shape so serious as to threaten the whole fabric with dissolution, and to leave a dark spot upon his memory. The Ronneberg Castle had soon been deserted by the pilgrims; they first wandered to Frankfort-on-the-Main, and then the Wetterau became their home. Here Marienborn and Herrnhaag were built up, and remained the seat of an active Moravianism until 1750.

The history of our people from 1744 to 1750 is characterized by much that is open to censure, but though the outpourings of a misguided religious enthusiasm marred, in a great measure, the fine structure that Zinzendorf had commenced, it finally ran its course and left some sterling results. This epoch is commonly known as the "*Sichtungs Zeit*," or "*Sifting Time*," and was marked by that overflow of fervor and devotional playfulness that gave the whole picture an air of monomania. Those unfortunate years, from 1744 to 1750, are strikingly recorded in the hymns, which, though expunged from the manuals of the Brethren almost a century ago, are still to be found in various hands.

Zinzendorf himself seems to have furnished the incentive to this departure from the spirit of a correct religious discipline, and was afterwards the foremost to discover the nature and real extent of his aberrations. He says: "The first opportunity for the terrible day of '*Sifting*' I myself must have given, and chiefly through the idea, ever present, and from which I never could emancipate myself during my whole life, that no state of true Christian felicity, no full reliance on Christ's death, could be realized unless the heart of the whole congregation assumed the disposition of a child. This idea became imprinted on me. On my return from America, I sought the opportunity of making it evident to my Brethren. It found ingress among them and was seized with avidity. But out of a few would-be children a large society sprung up, and this, in some years, sunk into a state of degeneracy. The source of those abuses arose from the views taken that converted the simplicity, uprightness, and candor of our worship into a matter of hilarity." One of the results of the "*Sifting Time*" was the desertion and final abandonment of Herrnhaag, which might be considered one of the finest towns of the early period, standing in view of the Ronneberg, and comprising nine hundred and fifty souls.

In this dispersion of Herrnhaag a better phase of Moravianism followed; its people emigrated in large numbers to America, and the departure from the memorable spot was signalized by hymns of sorrow, tears, and repentance. The place is now a scene of ruins, never having been resuscitated since 1750, but an inscription is still traced upon one of its dilapidated doors, significantly telling the story of its former devotion.

"Wir und des Lamms seine Blutgemein,
Woll'n unaufhörlich des Zeugen seyn,
Das im Opfer Jesu allein zu finden
Gnade und Freiheit von allen Sünden
Für alle Welt."

Among the descendants of the emigrants from Herrnhaag many curious reminiscences of its inner events are still preserved, and sometimes related, though with feelings of reserve and hesitation. Mixed up with the picture of a strange infatuation, there are, however, in the record of that gray past, numerous beautiful passages to which the old often and fondly recur.[1]

Before the full reinstatement of the Count as ecclesiastical head of Herrnhut, another deputation from the Saxon government, fully empowered to sift the doctrines of the Brethren, arrived and held council in the Castle of Hennersdorf. This committee of investigation, in which some of the ablest theologians were employed, was engaged fourteen days, and the result was satisfactory to the royal deputation, for the Brethren, by a public decree, were ac-

[1] The scenes of the Ronneberg, Herrnhaag, and the Wetterau are to be found depicted in a favorite work by Glaubrecht, "*Zinzendorf in der Wetterau.*"

knowledged as having henceforth the sanction of the law in all their proceedings and purposes.

A similar investigation was instituted in England, where a public petition brought them before the notice of Parliament. Long and warm debates succeeded, in which Lords Granville, Halifax, and Chesterfield, the Prince of Wales, and the Duke of Argyle, took part, arguing the tenets of the Moravians. The issue proved not only favorable, but the arguments closed with the strongest recommendations in their favor; the Bishop of Worcester adding his tribute of commendation to the people, their cause, and their remarkable history.

During this epoch, and, indeed, still later, similar prejudices induced the authorities in the American colonies to issue edicts against the Brethren, which lasted, however, but for a short time, and always reacted in their favor. Meanwhile, numerous small congregations had sprung up all around, which, grounded on the principles of Herrnhut, and endowed with all the Christian earnestness and warmth of the first Lusatian congregation, have outlived the tempests of time, and stand unscathed to this day.

The enlargement of the society, the increase of the missions, and all incidental disbursements, brought on, toward the year 1750, severe financial difficulties. The Count had, as we have seen, transferred the proprietorship of the estates of Berthelsdorf to his wife, who administered his property with great prudence and forethought. But through the connection of the Brethren with the Jew Gomez Serra, and many unjustifiable expenditures during the residence of the Count at the Lindsay House, in London, with his suite of fellow-laborers, called the Pilgrim Congregation, the troubles that came thickening upon him threatened to overwhelm him not only with bankruptcy, but even with imprisonment. He had, during the press of his pecuniary troubles, assumed the whole burden of the Brethren's obligations upon himself, and put his German estates under pledge for the final redemption of all debts incurred. But these would not have sufficed to meet all the liabilities that weighed upon them, had not the timely aid of devoted friends, and particularly those from Holland, come to the rescue.

During the first eight months of the year 1756, he resided in his own house at Berthelsdorf, where some of the best discourses of his later life were held, bearing the impress of that beautiful simplicity which betokened the "Disciple," the appellation now bestowed upon him by the flock that reverenced and loved him.

The death of the Countess, which occurred four years before his own, was a bereavement that fell heavily upon the Count; and although he found a second wife in Anna Nitschmann, who, in a spiritual sense, may have been able to take the place of the departed Erdmuth Dorothea, yet the position of the latter seems not to have been wholly filled by her successor.

With his newly married wife, his son-in-law De Watteville, and his daughters Benigna and Elizabeth, he now set out once more on a tour to Switzerland, passing through Barby, Marienborn, and Basle, and thence to Montmirail on Lake Neufchatel. Here he gathered a host of friends around him; thence he proceeded to Geneva and most of the principal Swiss towns; but feeling the symptoms of approaching disease, he hastened homeward, and reached Herrnhut early in the following year, 1758.

His final tour was made in 1759 to Holland, where he devoted his thoughts to the inner life of the true missionary, and spoke and wrote in the most expressive and artless language on the duties, obligations and aims of the faithful evangelist. In the same year, he received a friendly epistle from the Coptic Patriarch of Cairo, to which he responded in the most Christian terms, giving, in answer to his request, an account of the history and doctrines of the Brethren.

Although the life of the "Disciple" was now fast waning, yet his application to the cause of his people was unabated. During the last four months preceding his death, he held one hundred and twenty discourses, and he spoke, composed hymns and songs on themes which nourished his heart, almost up to his latest hours.

Zinzendorf's death occurred on the 9th of May, 1760, and the accompaniments of this event were characteristic of the people and customs of that day.

Lying calm and resigned on a low couch[1] in his house at Berthelsdorf, where he had dwelt during the early years of Herrnhut, he was visited in the closing hours of his illness by a large number of anxious friends, with whom he conversed to the last. The moments of his final departure cast that shadow of grief upon Herrnhut that was at all times peculiar to the sorrow of the older Moravian, a sorrow mixed with hope, a cloud illumined by sunshine.

His body lay for several days in the church at Herrnhut, where crowds came to visit it and to contemplate the earthly form of one whose presence, while living, infused its paternal tenderness among them all. To render the occasion impressive, music was performed during the whole time, six Brethren sitting around the corpse, who were relieved by six others every hour.[2] The funeral ceremonies were accompanied with all the impressive forms that distinguished the burials at Herrnhut; the body was borne to the cemetery by thirty-two of the clergy, who happened to be present, and had come from various parts of the world, sixteen sharing the office by turns. More than two thousand persons formed the procession, and as many more witnessed the scene as spectators. The final surrender of the

---

[1] The bedstead is preserved at Herrnhut.

[2] The performance of music during the exhibition of the remains was usual on extraordinary occasions. It formed a portion of the obsequies of Spangenberg, who lay in state at Berthelsdorf. (See Spangenberg.)

body to the earth was a moment of intense feeling, and long treasured up among the recollections of those who survived the memorable day.

In the archives of Herrnhut are still to be seen many of the memorials of Zinzendorf's life, illustrating his peculiarities of thought and habits, paintings of scenes in his family and his lineage, and portraits of nearly all his distinguished relatives. Among the relics deposited there and exhibited by one of his still surviving descendants, the archivist Von Schweinitz, is his Text-book, filled with pencil notes. This manual was his constant companion. The dignitary of the archives shows you, at the same time, the three lots held in a small case, which were carried in his vest pocket, and used on every occasion, where the will of the Lord was referred to. This species of communion with his divine Master was so blended with his character, that, like most individuals of a high spiritual cast, the whole outer seemed to be absorbed by an inner life. In applying his talents to spiritual themes, he became a sacred poet of a high order. His imagery and figures, though few, and limited to the purposes of a single and all-engrossing subject, are finely chosen, and, if we except the effusions of that short period when his music rioted in the puerilities of Herrnhaag and departed from decorum, his hymns have grown in the admiration of posterity through the lapse of the century that has now followed his death. Such was the facility with which he composed, that he frequently produced verses during church service, as the necessity of the occasion required; and he is known to have poured forth eight improvisations in a single day.

His sacred lyrics are published in a considerable volume, and are placed among the choicest German hymnology.[1] In these we find reflected Zinzendorf's own heart and being, his devotion, his reliance, his hope, his confidential intercourse with the

---

[1] Knapp, the able author of this compilation, who has ushered in the hymns of Zinzendorf with the most free and philosophical views on the true nature and essence of this department of composition, thus discourses upon his merits:

"No Christian poet could, at first sight, be less understood or less easily accepted by the reader, after turning aside from the ordinary church hymns in vogue, than Zinzendorf; and yet, in giving utterance to my own impressions, I could find no sacred bard who offers to the longing Christian a sweeter repast, a more glorious life-scene, or a richer acquisition. As the compiler of a hymnology, in the preparation of which I have perused myriads of hymns, I must honestly confess that no labor of my past life has been accomplished with such joyous results, such an abiding heavenly blessing, as the elaboration of those apparently unpoetical relics of this child-like man of the new Moravian covenant. I entered upon the work with some degree of diffidence; I had a preconceived idea of its monotony, and feared I should draw but poor results. But now, after it is closed, I look upon the sainted poet in quite another light. I give to the Christian world this book, as an *opus posthumum*, fully sensible how far I stand in heavenly wisdom below this lofty spirit, and how much I owe to God for having been allowed the high privilege of entering upon this work."

Saviour. All is concentrated in Christ, and his own relations to Him begin and terminate the great body of his hymns.[1]

Before entering into the memoirs of Zinzendorf, his portrait, as shown in correct and vivid delineations, furnishes an interesting study, being one of the most irresistible countenances found in man.[2] Without reading any written language in elucidation of those features, we peruse on their surface something that tells us their possessor must have cast superior influences around him, and that his mission on earth must have been truly remarkable.

In the sketch of Herrnhut, I have referred to the geniality that underlies the German character, and which is most obviously depicted in the portraiture of Zinzendorf. Here we read neither the ascetic nor the despairing and gloomy pietist, but the Moravian, as he discloses himself at the birth-day, the marriage, and the tomb. Such a life of love on the part of man, poured out constantly and freely among his fellow-men, we never observe in the history of ordinary philanthropy, and cannot account for it but on the principle of divine love,

---

[1] The best period of his hymns was 1722 to 1740, and his eccentricities occupy the interval of 1744 to 1749, during which there occurs an intermixture of various languages, bizarre comparisons and strange fancies.

[2] For a reliable portrait I would refer to Knapp's Hymns of Zinzendorf, in which is a copy of the painting from life, executed by Kupetsky, and formerly in possession of Lavater.

operating through man and permeating all his actions. That the whole world did not accept Zinzendorf, is a fact which renders his character and the tale of his life so much the more interesting. Coming out of a class of society from which few Christian apostles ever emerge, he was regarded as a strange phenomenon, and, from the originality of his manner, and the fearlessness of his course, in proclaiming Christ, his motives could not at all times be comprehended or entered into by society at large. To comprehend him and to enter into him, form the great distinctive contrasts of mind and heart, intellect and emotion, which I have proposed as the leading thought in the estimate of Zinzendorf, Herrnhut, and the Moravian character. Zinzendorf has, for a century past, been the subject of study, of portraiture, of idealisms, of poetical imitation, and of fiction. In all those attempts of philosophical and poetical minds to portray the being of pure devotion, the man of philanthropic love, of unalloyed faith, to borrow the tones of his harp and accommodate them to a more polished style of thought, the mind chiefly is called in play.

Goethe, whom I shall again have an opportunity of referring to, has adopted the Zinzendorfian worship to his purpose in this way, applying his art to a subject which he thoroughly comprehended, but out of which he could create no embodiment for his own soul. Herder, in his Adrastæa, holds up a spiritual image of Zinzendorf, and expatiates upon his hymns, as the production of a ductile language and filled with the riches of a heart-melody such as cannot elsewhere be found. Novalis, the sensitive but short-lived poet and philosophic novelist, born under a Moravian roof and nurtured in its usages, devoted much of his later life to Zinzendorf the poet, and Zinzendorf the divine.

Besides these names of wide repute and popularity, there is quite an array of writers, who took up the subject of Zinzendorf, æsthetically and philosophically; all regarding the subject from the stand-point of art, fiction, poetry or theological abstraction. But the entrance into Zinzendorf is given to minds of a different class from those idealists: it is approached by the medium of a purely emotional Christianity, and though the critic may imagine he knows, comprehends, and feels the self-same emotions as the "Disciple" knew and felt, he will find, upon a closer analysis, that he is yet afar off from him. None have given so full an interpretation of him and all the inner meanings that his hymns express, as the Moravian writers, who, divesting the matter of all rhetorical criticism, have employed the evangelical style itself, in which the "Disciple" thought, and seized the ideas in which he lived. Of such men I may name Gottfried Clemens and Bishop Albertini, as well as Schrauterbach, his early friend and companion.

It is worthy of note, that time has not cast its shadows over the memory of Zinzendorf, but appears to bring out in bolder relief the worth of his doctrines, and the beauty of his poetry. After the latter had lain in scattered fragments, some in the Brethren's hymn-books and some in manuscripts throughout the archives, for eighty years, the indefatigable compiler already quoted, assumed the work and gave to the notice of the world what it never knew it possessed.

These hymns have been adopted by other sects, and their imitations will be found in the collections of sister churches in this country, although their rendering in English is but an imperfect substitute for the original German thought and form of a Zinzendorfian theology.

In his personal appearance, Zinzendorf was dignified and commanded respect; but in the details of his attire, he showed great indifference and needed but a scanty wardrobe. He was generally averse to ostentation in the selection of his residence. The mansion now standing at Berthelsdorf, and known as the "Schloss," was, while he occupied it, but a modest building; and during a long time he retired into obscure and quiet quarters to pursue his meditations and work out the mission of his life. He rarely required attendants, and when he did, these were generally persons employed in other offices. All his income was devoted to the purposes of his cherished fondling, the church; and we are told by one of his most intimate, devoted, and loving friends, Bishop Hutton, of England, that his own personal expenses might have been covered by a yearly outlay of fifty pounds.

Of his consort, Erdmuth Dorothea, the biographer of Zinzendorf speaks in terms of the highest panegyric. Although she was the mother of twelve children, six sons and six daughters, she found time to take an active part in the spread of Moravianism and promulgation of the doctrines of the Brethren. During her husband's absence in America, we find her engaged in a mission to the Queen of Denmark, whom she visited at her castle of Hirschholm. She tried to divest her, as well as other potentates with whom she sought interviews, of the many misconceptions formed about Herrnhut and the Count, and upon this occasion found her a most accessible person, and cordial in her expressions and good wishes for the Countess and her cause.

A similar errand tempted her to visit Russia, and solicit a hearing from the empress, an enterprise which took place in winter. Her lots[1] decided, however, that she should not seek an audience of the empress, and disposing of her court-dress, she mounted her sledge and turned her back upon St. Petersburg. On reaching the borders of the empire, she received a summons to return, which she disobeyed.

[1] In those days every important step was submitted to and decided by lot, not only by Zinzendorf himself, but by all engaged in his cause.

Her whole life was a scene of activity either in the cause of Herrnhut and its people, or in the discharge of domestic duties. She was of a feeble frame, yet of great mental energy, uniting, at the same time, high intellectual powers with that extreme simplicity of thought and feeling, which distinguished so many female characters of her day in the Moravian church. She stood up ably and resolutely, full of counsel and resource, in the face of difficulty and amid all the embarrassments by which Zinzendorf found himself at times surrounded, and proved such an help-mate and heroic wife, in every sense of the word, that we need not wonder that his own eulogium on her character should be so strongly drawn. Her time, love, and affections being divided among her own family and her people, she was looked up to and regarded as a mother and a ruler. Of her numerous offspring, nearly all died in infancy and youth, (two of them during her absence in Russia,) and only three daughters survived her out of the twelve children.

Like so many distinguished personages of the early church, the Countess Erdmuth Dorothea possessed the gift of poesy in a remarkable degree, and her sacred lyrics rank with the ablest of those effusions which had their source in the Saviour's love, sufferings, and death; in the life, joy, and anticipations of Christian faith, in the whole Zinzendorfian sentiment and imagery, which forms the material of our hymns, and their essential ground-tone. Her compositions are characterized, at the same time, by a depth of conception and a finish in form which are not easily found in those of any other of her cotemporaries.

One year after the death of the Countess, Zinzendorf was united in marriage with Anna Nitschmann, and it is a somewhat singular coincidence in the lives of these two remarkable beings, that they lay on the bed of death at the same time and expired only within twelve days of each other. They had wandered together through the American forests; had consecrated the primitive log-cabin at Bethlehem, by a Christmas Eve solemnity; had assisted in many of the festivals of England, Marienborn, and Herrnhaag; had lived three years of wedded life; and were laid side by side in the tomb, in the central portion of the Hutberg, almost at the same time.

Anna Nitschmann was in many respects a remarkable personage, and attracted as much respect and deference from those who come under her immediate influence as Zinzendorf himself. She was the daughter of old Father Nitschmann,[1] one of those original emigrants from Moravia, who was present when the corner-stone was laid of the first church edifice in Herrnhut. His daughter Anna so distinguished herself by her piety and example, that at the age of fifteen years, the Sisters of Herrnhut

[1] He lies interred in the Bethlehem cemetery.

chose her their chief Eldress, in which capacity she drew upon herself the regard of the sisterhood of Herrnhut and Herrnhaag, at which latter place she resided during the Count's banishment from Lusatia. She was called the "Mother," and was one of those models of the old Moravian Sister, that have their living counterparts in Europe; but are here only preserved, either in portraits or in the memory. Like most of the early Moravians who were instrumental in building up the church, her life opened in rugged adversity. She, as well as her countrymen of Moravia, was inured to labor, and, when a girl, earned a livelihood by spinning wool. Besides possessing a poetical nature, which has left so many beautiful evidences behind, Anna Nitschmann was a speaker on public occasions, and although in those days it was required of all in unofficial life to speak and pray, yet for one of her sex she became eminent in the performance of ministerial duties. As Eldress, these abilities were called in constant requisition, the "*Advisers*," or those presiding over the choirs, being charged with the function of giving confidential advice and exhortation, as will be referred to under the head of the Moravian Cultus.

Nearly a century has elapsed since she and Zinzendorf have been consigned to the silent precincts of the Hutberg, and when that century comes round, we can fancy to ourselves the solemnities of the anniversary at Herrnhut, and the scene at the graves of the departed. These recollections are sacred there, and cannot be allowed to pass unnoticed, unfelt, and unwept.[1]

---

[1] The youthful Count Lynar, who spent some time at Herrnhut, and employed himself while there in the instruction of youth, was enabled to enter into the spirit of Zinzendorf and his institutions, and although not personally acquainted with him, has given us one of the best delineations of his character we possess. In a concise but able exposition of the Herrnhutian system and a general review of Moravian history up to his time, 1778, he thus speaks of Zinzendorf:—

"I have never seen the Count, but from his actions, his writings, and the testimony of judicious, credible, and unbiased observers, I have arrived at the following conclusions: He possessed genius, yet it was not universal, and only allowed its development under particular circumstances. It is a great error to suppose, as many do, that he would have become eminent, as minister of state, if he had remained in the discharge of civil pursuits. These require a moderate and guarded temperament; as soon as the passions are overcharged, the work they are engaged in is ruined. For the world, his address was too straightforward. He possessed talent, humor, and an extraordinary memory. His imagination was as lively and as glowing as was ever to be found in the human brain; it clung so closely to the subjects toward which it may have been led, that it pursued them into the very spheres, where they were finally lost. His mind was in a constant state of action and excitement. He formed a resolution so quickly, thought, spoke, and dealt with so much decision, that there never seemed to be any doubt, objection, or hindrance underlying it. He availed himself of various languages, in order to give readiness to his ideas. Had he addicted himself to more cautious reflection, he might have escaped the charge of manifold contradictions, and saved himself the trouble of rendering so many explanations, and writing so many defenses.

"That his judgment was not so weak as many are inclined to believe, is fully corroborated by the numerous correct and rare views he has taken of the wants of his times. He was true, honest and sincere; qualities which, aided by his humor, often served to render his expressions naive and striking. Bold and undaunted in the face of danger, he seems to have chosen for his motto, 'tu contra audentior ito.' In this regard, he resembled Luther. That ambition was his chief incentive, and, as one of his nearest female kindred imputed to him, that he sought the highest seat in the realm of humility, I do not believe.

"Whether, in the course of long and uninterrupted success in the realization of so many of his plans and the surmounting of every difficulty, some feelings of self-adulation may have softly entered into his heart, and even when rendering to God the glory, the gentle thought of self may have stolen in and got the upper hand, I will not pretend to say, although his tone and even occasional personal acknowledgments in his writings would tend to show something of this within him. But his ruling passion and the source from which all his actions flowed were, in my view, his love of Jesus Christ, and a burning desire to promote the happiness of mankind.

"From his early youth he sought no pleasure but that of spiritual pursuits, and this remained the absorbing object of his life. Some of the circumstances of his education may have given rise to this, yet, disregarding the influences of immediate causes and looking to a higher hand, which guides and controls all beneath it; weighing the various and widely disseminated benefits imparted to both church and state by the exertions of Count Zinzendorf, and the bulwark they have established for the Christian and good citizen against vice and infidelity, I cannot but regard this branch of the work, as well as the great work itself, as one brought about by Divine agency, wherein the human instrument himself is endowed with many imperfections.

"Selfishness could never be imputed to Count Zinzendorf. All that was his own he gave away freely, and, in every enterprise, he never considered from what source money was to come. 'It must be done,' he would say; 'I shall continue to borrow, if even tons of gold are required. I expend nothing on myself, but all for the use of the congregation. God will see it paid.' It often involved him in difficulties, but he always extricated himself. No one could have carried industry to greater lengths. He slept but a few hours, and allowed himself barely time to eat. To write and preach so much, to perform so many journeys, to erect so many schools, set them in operation and continue them, required a more than ordinary activity.

"Out of all that has been said of him, we may draw one leading trait in his character, and that was immoderation. He pursued everything to its farthest limits. He no sooner caught the shadow of a possibility than it grew into a probability, and that became a certainty, and upon this latter he acted. Dark fancies, but in harmony with his genius and incitements, worked with remarkable force upon his mind, summoned up all his energies and directed them to the purposes he had in view. Under this form, he possessed a fervor which bore him successfully through many undertakings. I might here apply to his case the figure of a lover in contrast with a friend, who are each in earnest pursuit of some desirable object. While one is warm, the other glows; where one sees insuperable difficulties, the other wastes no time in reflection; while one is taking soundings, the other has leapt into the water. While the friend walks, the lover runs, wanders, stumbles, falls; runs again, and, finally, reaches his object." (*Lynar, Ursprung und Fortgange der Brüder Unität.*)

In further illustration of the preceding characterization of Zinzendorf, I add the following specimen of his intercourse with children, which is to be found among his discourses entitled "Kinder Reden," and although an English translation will not do justice to the childlike simplicity which enabled him to convey Christ's being and attributes among children, still it may serve as a substitute for the use of such as are not versed in the language in which these innocent sentiments are delivered.

"Our dear Saviour says, Forgive and ye shall be forgiven. As soon as a child has sufficient understanding to know that another one has done something to him that he thinks is not right, or something which he does not like, and takes it amiss, and is much affronted, then our dear Saviour also takes it very much amiss of him. But when you are so friendly disposed to one another, that you are satisfied with everything that passes between you; when your friend is sorry for what he has done, and you feel sorry for him on account of it and you say nothing more about it, but become affectionate to one another, then your Saviour also forgives you.

"My son, give me thy heart! My children, I have spent much time in thinking what should prevent every one from giving up his heart to his Creator, why every one is not happiest in company with his Creator. Cannot all eat and drink and dress in the same manner as others do, and yet love their Creator? God says, in Jeremiah, something similar to this: 'Thy father hath eaten and drunk and loved me, and thou thinkest, when thou art king, thou canst not love me. It is well with him, but with thee it is not.'

"My dear children! see that your hearts are given up to your Saviour, and promise him that you will be his. Say to Him, Dear Saviour, Thou seest and knowest me and all my wants, and knowest best where my danger lies. Come, against my own wishes, to my assistance. Save me from misfortune; support me, a poor child; Thou seest that I cannot make my own happiness, make Thou it for me. Our dear Saviour will not leave your prayers unheard, when they proceed from the heart," etc.

V.

SPANGENBERG, OR MORAVIANISM ILLUSTRATED.

It was on the 17th of November, 1727, that Count Zinzendorf passed through Jena, and had an interview with Doctor Buddeus and some of the students of the University. Among these was August. Gottlieb Spangenberg, born in Klettenberg, in 1704, and residing here, engaged in study. The Count, as usual, entertained the company with those matters nearest his heart, dwelling upon the passage from Corinthians: "Be ye, therefore, followers of God, as dear children." He took occasion to describe the new Zion, Herrnhut, to them, which was now just entering its fifth year. Our young student was strongly drawn toward Zinzendorf; his feelings were awakened by his manner, his subject, and the picture he drew of the colony in Lusatia; but at this time he entered into no further acquaintance with the Count.

The following year, the deputation sent from Herrnhut to England, consisting of three Brethren, passed through Jena, and renewed the friendship with Doctor Buddeus and the Jena students. Spangenberg was delighted to see them, bade them welcome, and translated into the Latin language the address they were conveying to the English court. There was a general awakening among the Jena students about this time, and an active correspondence sprung up with Zinzendorf and Herrnhut, particularly on the part of Spangenberg, who prevailed on the former to repeat his visit to Jena, where he told him he would find the sympathies of more than one hundred students strongly inclining to him and his people. Responding to the call, he went once more to Jena, and there, in the little fervent assemblage, they sang, "Salve Crux beata, Salve!" This event resulted in a visit of Spangenberg and Clemens to Herrnhut, in 1730, where their own reception, the life of the people, the warmth of their apostolic love, their singularly resolute spirit to abide by their faith, and resist the persecutions of government and of society, made a profound impression on the two students, and decided the future course of life of the Magister of Jena. In 1732 he received an appointment to Halle, as adjunct professor and superintendent of the Orphan House. His participation in the cause of Herrnhut and Zinzendorf soon drew down upon him the animadversions of the Theological faculty there, with Professor Franke at its head, who called him to task for his zeal and his manner of carrying out, too literally, the doctrines of Christ and his Apostles. Among other complaints brought against him was that of having performed the ceremony of washing of feet. He answered that a weary soldier had called on him for aid, whom he took into his house, and having bruised feet, he applied warm water to them to heal them. The learned professor informed him that such an act was beneath his dignity, as one of the learned faculty; that Christ never intended that the *pedilavium* should be taken in its literal sense, nor actually applied by his disciples or mankind to the washing of feet. Spangenberg's reply was very much in character with his whole life and in accordance with a true interpretation of the Moravian tenets. He requested that a child should be called in and have the passage read to him respecting this transaction of the Saviour, and then ask him the purport of it. What the child's answer should be, was the answer to the question in dispute. He held himself as wise as the child, but no wiser.

Laboring under all this opposition, he found his position as professor and director of the Orphan House irreconcilable with his sense of duty, as he conceived himself called upon to preach to mankind; and when a decree was sent him from his sovereign to vacate his office, which, rather than to deplore, he hailed with joy, as it was a pleasure to suffer for conscience' sake. Returning to Jena, he was received with acclamation by his old friends, the students, who escorted him out of the city, when he departed for Herrnhut.

The two friends met once more, and when Spangenberg laid a statement of his grievances before

Zinzendorf, both concluded to refer to the Brethren's general council as to what course should be pursued. Spangenberg asked whether he had not better publish a defence of himself before the eyes of the Halleasians and the world. The conclusion on the part of the Brethren was couched in that one highly characteristic sentence used in all similar cases: "Remain silent and wait upon the Lord." Having now become an inmate of this cherished abode, he soon turned his attention to the new enterprise of the Brethren, the mission to the West Indies, and departed with four married couples and ten Brethren, on foot, to Copenhagen, to see them embark thence on this new and hazardous adventure.

The project of sending out missions to Georgia was conceived and carried out in 1735, and to Spangenberg was assigned the task of leading the little band of Brethren on this perilous expedition. He himself proceeded to London, and was joined by the company of emigrants soon after. During his stay he made an acquaintance with the commissioners for Georgia, as well as with the Bishop of London; with the former, his time was spent in negotiations preparatory to the emigration and settlement of the colony, and his object in calling on the latter was, to lay before him the history of Herrnhut and the schemes of its founder.

After a speedy voyage, Spangenberg arrived in the new and thinly peopled province of Georgia, and took possession of the fifty acres of land granted him by the trustees in London, and with the little body of ten persons, commenced building a hut on the Savannah River. Previously to its erection, they encamped fourteen days in the open air, beside a fire, felling trees, out of which they split rude boards; and scarcely had they completed the humble dwelling and moved in, before a storm of rain came on. As there was another arrival of twenty more Brethren looked for the following year, preparations were forthwith made for the erection of a larger house for their reception.

Hither in the wilderness, in a foreign country, Herrnhut and its observances, its hymns and its prayers, were soon transplanted; and as a relief to the labors of the woodman's life, which it really proved to these people, the petition and the anthem went up to heaven at all hours. The Halle professor was now obliged to wield the axe, prostrating the trees of a dense pine forest, and hewing timber for the construction of houses. He aided in cooking food, and left untouched no branch of labor wherein he found call for his services and ingenuity. In February of 1736, the twenty emigrants arrived from Herrnhut, which place they had left the preceding August. They came under the conduct of Bishop David Nitschmann, Governor Oglethorpe and John Wesley having been their fellow-passengers. General Oglethorpe, who was governor of Georgia, often came to see Spangenberg and his colony, and, on such occasions, found him engaged in work, and sometimes employed as cook. Wesley's acquaintance with Spangenberg originated here, and the friendship between the former and the Brethren continued until 1740, when he instituted the society afterwards known as the Methodists.

Under the superintendence of Bishop David Nitschmann, a regular organization of Herrnhutian life was now commenced on a very small scale, having its overseers, admonishers, and its servants and nurses. The minor subdivisions, known at Herrnhut as the "Bands," and afterwards common in England, were also introduced, in which a few met together for the purpose of spiritual edification and prayer. Anton Seiffert was then appointed Elder, and entered upon his office with the benediction of the bishop; who, laying his hands upon him, prayed fervently for the success of his ministration. Seiffert received his consecration under the deepest impressions, and in silence; and then, with the usual accompaniments of hymns of praise, ended that remarkable scene in the Georgia forests.

Spangenberg now turned his attention to Pennsylvania. A company of Schwenkfelders, who had gone out from Berthelsdorf to America, had directed their course to this province and settled here. He was desirous of seeking them, and examining their condition; and, accordingly, setting out by sea for Charleston, and thence again by sea to New York, he arrived at the latter place in safety, after a twelve days' voyage from the former. He traveled across New Jersey into Pennsylvania, and discovered the Schwenkfeld colony settled in that portion of the province now known as Montgomery County; and was hospitably received by one of them named Christopher Wiegner. Very soon, however, he received the appointment from Bishop Nitschmann to proceed to the West Indies, on a visitation to the mission in St. Thomas. He consented to go, and repairing without delay to New York, embarked for St. Thomas, on the 10th of September, 1736. Remaining in St. Thomas and St. Croix, until the sixteenth of October, and reviving the drooping missionaries there, who had many difficulties to contend with, not only in the climate, but in the opposition of the white inhabitants, who covered them with persecution and insult, he again set sail for New York, with the well-known Nicolas Garrison, who proved a warm friend, and sympathized deeply with the Christian errand he was engaged in. Returning to his friend Wiegner and the Schwenkfelders, he remained among them until a summons came to him from Bishop Nitschmann to proceed to Georgia, where his presence was anxiously awaited by the colony. They were in difficulties. The Spaniards were endeavoring to supplant the English colonists, who demanded the assistance of the Moravians. These refused to take up arms in their defence, and saw no other prospect before them, but to forsake their flourishing little settlement, and emigrate farther North. This event soon followed; the colony near Savannah was broken up; the last Brethren remaining there departed for Pennsylvania, and Spangenberg, after a four years' arduous, zealous, and tempest-tossed service in America, proceeded to Philadelphia, and embarked thence for Europe. He only learned after his embarkation on the vessel, that she had no means of defence; that a war had actually broken out between England and Spain, and that the voyage was likely to be the most perilous he had yet undertaken. Under the weight of emotion inspired by these circumstances, he quoted to himself that passage of Scripture, "And when ye hear of wars and rumors of wars, be ye not afraid," and his heart was strengthened. The voyage, however, proved prosperous; he landed safely in England, and, toward the close of 1739, he found himself in Marienborn, the seat of the Brethren at that period. In this last voyage, as well as in that from Philadelphia to Georgia, which occupied eleven weeks, Spangenberg's equanimity and perfect dependence on God were illustrated in a remarkable degree. In the first voyage, the passage was so stormy and his apparent indifference so great, that the captain regarded him in a superstitious light; he looked on him as a sorcerer, and was on the point of casting him overboard, and several times declared himself to that effect. On his voyage to England, his calmness and inner peace were so striking, that he drew around him the more alarmed of his fellow-passengers, who seemed to find protection in his mere presence. At Marienborn he was united in marriage with the widow Immig, whom Zinzendorf and the Countess had known at Dresden, and who was an exemplary Eldress in her Choir during the time of her widowhood.

Spangenberg's scene of activity was now chiefly in England, where, during the absence of Zinzendorf in America, in 1741 and 1742, he was engaged in spreading the name and doctrine of Herrnhut among the English people; and numbers were found who were touched with the earnestness and sincerity of our active apostle, joined the new cause he was endeavoring to make known, and perpetuated the church in a land where their descendants live in the profession and enjoyment of Moravianism to the present day. At one time we find him holding an interview with the Archbishop of Canterbury, and pressing the claims of the new church upon his notice and protection; at another time returning to Marienborn and looking after the interests of the congregation there. An extensive correspondence was kept up all this time with Count Zinzendorf; which continued until the return of the latter from America, in 1743. Having, in 1744, been consecrated bishop, it was deemed expedient that Spangenberg should now revisit America; and setting sail with his wife on a day when the daily text read, "I am with you," he reached New York once more, after a passage that was accompanied by much apprehension, the sea then being infested with Spanish vessels. Once more within that new and distant country, his attention was directed to the Indians; and he repaired to Shekomeko, with his wife and Captain Garrison. From Shekomeko they proceeded to Bethlehem; where they remained for five years, arranging and superintending the Economy of the Brethren there, as well as at Nazareth, Christianspring, and Gnadenthal. This social plan was upheld for twenty years in these several places, and was, for the greater part of that time, under Spangenberg's direction and care. Their joint population at this early period was about six hundred, among whom there were probably a number of converted Indians.

No explanation having been given of the principles of the Moravian Economy, as it existed in this country during those twenty years, when it stood under the supervision of Spangenberg, a few words might be added in its elucidation, particularly since some misconstruction has been placed upon the subject by those who have taken a superficial view of our history and character. The motto of this common family was, "In commune oramus, in commune laboramus, in commune patimur, in commune gaudemus."[1] Under Spangenberg's administration, it was conceded to every one that the property he held, previously to entering the common circle, was to be retained; his labor only was bestowed on the com-

[1] "We pray together, we labor together, we suffer together, we rejoice together."

mon cause. How labor itself was regarded, how it was sanctified, how it was accompanied with demonstrations of festivity, with prayers and song, has already been shown. The whole element of self had to be merged in the exclusive desire and aim of the Brethren to promulgate the knowledge of Christ. No one, therefore, labored for the accumulation of earthly treasure; but life, and all that renders it a drudgery to us of a later stage of thought and action, was one continued preparation for the unseen kingdom of spiritual joys.

During its infancy, and indeed the greater part of its maturity, this social family flourished in love and harmony; and the picture which Spangenberg himself gives us of it during 1744 to 1749, is such as must lead us to believe that it was the realization of all that is dreamt of by men, who make a similar attempt, but on a materialistic basis. What became of self and all its impressions during this period, or how the jarrings of human discord were hushed for so long a time, has never been chronicled to us; but if we enter into the Christian life, festive joys, and industrious avocations of these early, primitive people, we can find a solution of the problem, why the system was upheld so long. The tendency to accumulate, which belongs to all systems of socialism, and proves their eventual downfall, was excluded from the Moravian Economy; which is evident from the very fact that its united co-operation was a labor of love. Its profits and its surplus were expended in supporting the schools, in aiding the neighboring and destitute Indians, who often came to Bethlehem for food and shelter, in sending out missionaries and teachers among them, and in receiving emigrants from abroad. To do all this, and the work was not a small one, the most unremitted labor was demanded; and in this labor all were engaged, the young and old; so that it necessarily called down upon itself the character of a species of adoration.

It was during these five years that Spangenberg found all his powers called into activity. He managed the whole Economy of the Brethren, established schools to the number of thirty, instituted new congregations, and, in addition to all this, now devoted his attention to the Indians. In 1749 we find Spangenberg once more departing for Europe, where he arrived after a remarkably quick voyage of four weeks. During the following year he passed his time in England and Germany alternately, going constantly to and fro; and engaged with Zinzendorf in conducting the affairs of the Brethren. His faithful wife, Mary, was called away from him in 1751, shortly before his intended departure for Greenland, whither he was summoned. He gives us, in his own language, a pathetic account of the end of her days on earth; and in the memoir read by the Ordinarius, (Zinzendorf,) who himself drew up the eulogy on her character, there is a fine portrayal of all the eminent qualities that marked Mary Spangenberg, in common with those rare women who took the lead in the spiritual ministration of the early Moravians. She, like the Countess of Zinzendorf and Anna Nitschman, was ready to officiate on all occasions; and in speaking of her loss, Zinzendorf deploringly regarded it as an irreparable one.

Brother Joseph, as our Bishop Spangenberg was now affectionately called,[1] departed for Copenhagen, to set sail for Greenland; but being too late to embark, his mission was frustrated, and he returned to Herrnhut. In the same year he again left Europe for America; and, after a pleasant voyage of eleven weeks, during which time he edified his fellow passengers with daily service, singing, and composing hymns for them, and once furnishing them a Love-Feast, he arrived in New York, and forthwith proceeded to the bourne of his wishes, Bethlehem. He found the congregation much larger; and in the discharge of his duties as Patriarch, to which station he was chosen immediately on his arrival, he found himself surrounded with difficulties. Here and there he discovered some loosened chords of harmony; and to bind them fast again became his constant care and solicitude.

Lord Granville having offered the Brethren a tract of land in South Carolina, comprising 100,000 acres, Bishop Spangenberg set out, the 25th of August, 1752, with five assistants, to discover its locality and

[1] And as he signed himself. See MS. of the Historical Society of Pennsylvania, printed in Reichel's History of Nazareth Hall, page 9.

survey it. The text for the day of their departure was, "The people that knoweth its God," etc.

The march of the exploring party through Virginia and North Carolina was attended with difficulties that no one had imagined. They had morasses and forests to traverse and mountains to climb, and were forced to encamp every night, for fourteen weeks, in the woods. For paths through these inaccessible forests they sought out the track of the buffalo, and frequently relieved their horses of their baggage, in order to enable them to climb the steep rocky ascents. Winter came on, and they found themselves wading through deep snows amid these impenetrable American wilds. On one occasion their food as well as provender for the horses became exhausted; and they spent three days without eating, when, coming upon a little brook, they followed its course into an open pasture, where they shot two deer. A short distance hence they came in contact with white people, who conducted them to the region afterwards known as the Wachau.[1]

It was not until the 12th of February following that Spangenberg once more found himself safely seated in Bethlehem, recounting the adventures of his heroic mission among the solitudes of North Carolina. Early in the spring of 1753 he delivered an admirable discourse in the Brethren's Church;

---

[1] Now the country around Salem, North Carolina, and called Wachovia.

then once more embarked on board of a ship, and arrived in London on the 27th of May.

During the month of April of the ensuing year, we again find him celebrating Easter morning on the ocean, and calling to mind the multitudes it had swallowed up, and who should all rise again "in that great day of the Lord." This was his fourth visit to America, and lasted seven years. On this occasion he was welcomed by the people of Bethlehem with a Love-Feast. Shortly after his arrival he was married to the widow Miksch, whom he had known as a handmaid of Christ, the usual appellation of all the faithful and exemplary women of those days, and he speaks of her in these terms: "My Martha is a good child, a worthy gift of the Saviour for me! If her open-heartedness and my sternness could be divided between us, it would be of service to the Church. We yield ourselves up to it."

The year 1755 was the opening of Indian troubles for the Moravians of Bethlehem, and they were thrown into perplexity and peril through the operation of opposite causes. From their well-known zeal for the Indians, many of these believed them to be their friends, and fled to their towns for protection. Many of the white inhabitants, on the other hand, regarded them as being in league with the savages, and an attack on their part threatened them more than once. But when the appalling massacre on the Mahony became known, the character of the Brethren came out in its true light; and the illusion was dispelled that they were allies of the Indians and French against the English. Early in the morning after the night of this memorable catastrophe, Spangenberg called the congregation, and after reading the text for the day, he detailed the circumstances of the sad event, the news of which had just been brought by the messenger to Bethlehem; then hastening to Nazareth he repeated the mournful tale of the massacre of the eleven Brethren of the Pilgrim House at Gnadenhütten. To form some idea of the fearful state of Bethlehem at this time, I will quote the following lines from Spangenberg's letter to Zinzendorf: "The Indians are now threatening to attack Bethlehem, but our hearts rest in childlike hope. Our children are ignorant of the war and murder around them; they are all lively, and sing and play before the Lord in their innocence. The widows and single sisters are like the children, although they hear of the massacres and burnings. The married sisters look upon their children and infants, and suffer their tears to flow over them, yet they are quite gentle and resigned. The Brethren are day and night on the watch to guard against an attack. The neighboring people seek refuge among us, and we refuse no one. In short, we are comforted and resolute in the Lord.

"We abide, unterrified, at our posts; for should we yield, the whole country between this and Philadelphia would become a prey to the ravages of the Indians, there being no other place that could resist them. As yet no one has deserted us; indeed it has not entered the mind of any to seek for safety outside of our people. From man we seek no rescue; the Lord alone, whose property we are, will aid us. How tender is our mutual love under these circumstances! When we behold a brother, it is like looking upon an angel of God. The sisters pray, weep, and comfort us with their childlike and placid looks. Some repining words are now and then heard uttered by one or the other, but she is soon reminded;—Have not we a Saviour, who loves us tenderly? a Father, who numbers all the hairs in our heads? a Holy Spirit, that cares for the body when it lies in the earth, until it is again raised up? God be praised, we have thus far spilled no blood, and think not of doing it. We are good children together, and if we are industrious, life and things prosper."

The letter is not only characteristic of Brother Joseph himself, but is the best illustration that I am able to adduce of Moravian faith in the middle of the last century, among the most trying events in which it was placed.

It will be seen by these statements, that the whole country north of Philadelphia was, in a manner, shielded by these little Moravian settlements, and that their protection lay more in the strength of the spiritual calmness and heavenly peace, that imparted such a remarkable and inspiring personality to Zinzendorf and Spangenberg on the stormy ocean, than in any material means of defence.[1] The provincial governor, who then resided at Philadelphia, became a warm friend of Spangenberg, and fully appreciated the valuable services of the Brethren. He availed himself of the bishop's counsel, and regarded these people as one of the outposts of civilization during those stormy periods.

Spangenberg's energies were now tried to their utmost capacity; he not only had the whole supervision of the several Economies, but kept up an active correspondence with Germany and the West Indies, as well as with North Carolina.

Of the Indians who had taken refuge among the Moravians, there were in Bethlehem one hundred, whose necessities were provided for, in being nursed, fed, and clothed. During the winter, the greater part of these were lodged in one house, but when summer returned little huts were provided for them. During the year 1756 the number of refugees who sought this asylum numbered six hundred. These, with much difficulty, were carried through a severe winter by the Brethren. Some flying to them naked, were provided with clothing, others nearly starved were served with food, while to all was dispensed the bread of life; as they not only made it a point to

[1] In each of the Moravian settlements of Bethlehem, Nazareth, Christianspring, Gnadenthal and Friedensthal, there was a regular night-watch kept; and a large number were armed, who frequently went out on scouting expeditions to discover Indians in ambush around the villages.

provide for their physical wants, but preached the gospel, and sung the hymns of Herrnhut for them.

It may well be imagined that this outpouring of generosity exhausted the means of the Moravians. Some subsidies were sent from other parts, as Philadelphia and intermediate places, but to sustain themselves under these trying circumstances, they found it incumbent to strive "in body and spirit."

In the year 1759 Bishop Spangenberg undertook a second journey to North Carolina, which, seven years before, accompanied by his surveyor, his hunter, and fellow-pilgrims of Bethlehem, he had ventured to explore. With his wife and a few Brethren, he now departed, and his adventures on this expedition were nearly as bold as were the first, in 1752. The Indians were as hostile in those portions of the province as they had been in Pennsylvania in 1755 to 1757. They burned and massacred throughout North Carolina and Virginia, and our party having to encamp in the woods every night, their lives stood in imminent danger. The journey was accompanied with such peril that no guide could be procured to conduct them through the forest, but when near the region of the Wachau, they succeeded in sending a messenger before them to the people of Bethabara, who immediately came out with an escort to meet them. They found the place surrounded by the same dangers that but a few years before had encompassed Bethlehem. The wild Cherokees were lurking around, and the utmost vigilance of the inhabitants was exercised night and day to ward them off. They were obliged to sustain all who came to them for protection; and they had one hundred children under twelve years of age to care for. Brother Joseph remained eleven months in the Wachau, and amid all the dangers of Indian strife, he was deeply engaged in arranging the internal affairs of Bethabara, directing its people in ritual and doctrine, and establishing its family in faith and love. The return to Bethlehem was amid the haunts of the savage. At night a fire was kindled in the woods, around which while some slept, others watched; but an unerring hand finally conveyed them unscathed to Bethlehem, after a journey of twenty-four days. They were again welcomed home, and their arrival was signalized by a Love-Feast of the whole congregation. It was four years previous to this that Spangenberg had been apprised of the death of the Countess Zinzendorf; and now, in 1768, the still more afflicting news of the Count's own departure were brought to Bethlehem. Bishop Joseph's sentiments on both occasions are so beautifully couched in his native German, that I refrain from the attempt to render their untranslatable pathos in our own language. He has, both here and elsewhere, drawn the finest psychological portrait of Erdmuth Dorothea von Zinzendorf that we possess; and his eulogium on the "Disciple" himself, at receiving the intelligence of his death, is so Moravian in its tone and expression, that the original language in which it is conveyed is its most proper medium for perusal.

At the time the news of Zinzendorf's death came to America, a second visit had been anxiously looked for; he had secured such a firm hold on the affections of all, that his presence seemed needed everywhere; and it was a source of profound grief that both this hope was to be left unrealized and that the great spiritual patriarch was no longer to be seen on this side of eternity. In many an old Moravian this transition of a friend from one life to the other produced no visible effect—it became a matter of time only when spirit should again become united to spirit, and the affections of earth be renewed again in heaven.

Soon after the death of the "Disciple," Spangenberg was recalled to Europe to assume the place the loss had made vacant; and he accordingly prepared for this event by a general visitation to the congregations around Bethlehem. The Economy at this place, having now lasted twenty years, was dissolved; and in a Love-Feast which was given in celebration of his departure, he imparted his blessings to all his people, and consigned them to the keeping of the Saviour. He was accompanied to Philadelphia by a few friends, who returned soon after with his final salutation to his American Brethren, conveyed in the same scriptural terms of simplicity and affection that characterized all his writings and discourses. To render these discourses in an English dress, does so little justice to their author, and serves to make Moravianism such an incomprehensible thing, that I forbear here, as elsewhere, placing Spangenberg before the reader, whenever his warmest effusions are called forth. In common with Zinzendorf, his thoughts were born of the language of his country, his religious emotions were the offspring of the national temperament, and when we attempt to make our own tongue the medium of the Moravian ideas of an earlier day, we can give them no adequate expression.

After a tempestuous voyage of sixty-nine days to England, and another nearly disastrous one of five weeks thence to Hamburg, he found himself once more approaching Herrnhut, after thirteen years' absence. He entered the church at nine o'clock in the evening, without any previous notice of his arrival, just as the congregation was singing, "O Haupt voll Blut und Wunden." His figure and general appearance had a striking resemblance to that of the "Disciple," and the assembly were so affected with this sudden apparition that many shed tears. The next morning he repaired to the grave of Zinzendorf on the Hutberg, to drop a tear upon the spot where his nearest earthly friend now lay interred.

Spangenberg was immediately appointed a member of the Conference of Herrnhut, to which was confided the general direction of the church, both at home and abroad, and which, in 1769, assumed, under an enlarged form, the title of "The Unity's

Elders' Conference." Through his later years his mental activity was as great as ever, and in addition to all his other ministerial engagements, he was employed in writing several important works, among which were the Life of Zinzendorf and his celebrated Idea fidei Fratrum. The former furnishes the most correct and authentic biography we have of Zinzendorf; the latter treatise attracted much attention throughout Europe, having been translated into the English, Dutch, Danish, French, and Swedish languages. A great portion of this time was spent in Barby, where the Unity's Conference held its seat for the period of thirteen years; and on his arriving at his eighty-first birth-day, the anniversary happening to fall upon the Jubilee of his official years spent in the service of the United Brethren, it was solemnized with all the demonstrations of joy befitting such a memorable occasion. He was awakened early in the morning by a choir of singers: his colleagues of the Conference expressed their hearty good wishes, and congratulated him on the event of the day, on the wonderful preservations that had been shown him in his eventful career, and the hale old age to which he had attained, the fidelity he had shown, and the success that had crowned all his works on earth. They prayed that a succession of blessings might descend upon his declining days, and that he might grow more and more in grace until his race was run. In reply to these expressions of love on the part of his associates, he made the most candid confessions, acknowledged his gratitude to his God and Saviour, and closed the scene by kneeling down with them all, and pouring out his soul in fervent prayer. Hymns composed for the occasion were handed him by numerous friends, and during the Love-Feast prepared for him a special psalm was sung, in commemoration of the day, and performed by choir and orchestra, according to custom. After the celebration had ended, he presented a written address to the Brethren who had joined in it, wherein, among other things, he promised to prepare and present to them, as a keepsake, a narration of all the wonderful blessings which God had conferred upon them since the opening of their history.

Brother Joseph remained in the full possession of his mental powers, performing all the duties assigned him, until near the close of his remarkable and eventful life. His second faithful spouse was taken from him in 1789, in her eighty-first year—a worthy handmaid of Christ, having shared in all the vicissitudes of her husband's life, dispensed the charities and benevolence of her own peculiar calling to every one with whom she came in contact, and left behind her a name precious to all. During the Bishop's latter days, when disease began to show its inroads, he removed from Herrnhut to the Unity's mansion at Berthelsdorf, known as the "Schloss." Here he was shown many attentions by those around him; but though his bodily powers gave way, his active mind was engaged to the last moment. On a fine morning, in the month of August, he allowed himself to be carried out into the field, where the reapers were taking off the harvest. He summoned them around him, gave them refreshments, addressed and blessed them. Then, raising his feeble voice, sang, "Nun danket alle Gott," which so affected the assembled group that their tears flowed freely, and the scene of the Patriarch's last farewell never faded from their memories. At the age of eighty-eight years his life finally closed in a gentle slumber, through which he was permitted to derive some glimmerings of heaven, in the shadowy images that flitted before him, ere he closed his eyes forever on earth.

Beautiful as his death, were the last observances paid to his interment. His remains lay exposed to view in the chapel at Berthelsdorf, and were visited by all the people of Herrnhut and its environs; soft music and solemn hymns performing their dirge-like harmony during the exhibition of the body, as was wont on all great occasions. Then it was borne to the Herrnhut Cemetery, where it now reposes among so many more of the good and the truly great.

In following up the career of another artless and devoted man, my aim has chiefly been to illustrate Moravianism, by furnishing the biography of one of its best representatives and exponents. All that Spangenberg has performed, — all that he has preached, written, and sung, (for his hymns, like Zinzendorf's, are replete with the one great theme of Christ's love and sacrifice,)—elucidate in their own peculiar and engaging light the whole spirit of Moravian life. Not only the every-day social life can be gathered here in these memoirs, but the martyrdom of the people, whose history is included in it, nearly up to the close of the last century—its most marked and eventful epoch. Such untiring zeal and unfaltering devotion in the cause of his Master was only equaled, not excelled, by the "Disciple" himself; and in the memoirs that have been left, drawn chiefly from his own papers, there is nothing to show but perfect consistency in the whole course of his life and Christian mission. His career was uniformly pure and self-sacrificing; he was at all times ready to yield to the calls of his people, going to and fro, wherever summoned. In his devotion, his lamp was always trimmed and burning, and in his solicitude for his flock, he was ready with words of reproof, correction, advice, and comfort, at all times and at all places. As a man and a Christian, he is a striking pattern among the remarkable men who were instrumental in building up the renewed church of the Brethren.

VI.

THE MORAVIAN CULTUS.

THE nature of the Moravian Cultus, or mode of worship, forms, and rituals, may be partly inferred from the brief sketch I have given of Herrnhut; but, in addition to this, it demands some general and abstract views, taken from a stand-point without the pale of the society. I have avoided entering into many details of the religious organization of Herrnhut; as the Moravianism of America forms the engrossing subject of these pages, and the picture of its German prototype has only been introduced in order to furnish the origin of its forms and customs, and, thereby, to elucidate their spirit.

Before regarding the picture of the festive institutions, as they exist in Europe, and still, in some degree, characterize the Moravian rural villages in this country, I must premise, that the same distinctions of age and sex as those in Herrnhut were strictly preserved in the religious arrangements of Moravian life and worship. To each of these divisions, or "Choirs," was reserved its appointed times and places of inculcation, devotion, and festivity; for between these three avocations, life, spiritually speaking, was divided. Children, youth, and adults of either sex, and the married collectively, were divided into distinct classes, who, although all assembling together on general church occasions every Sunday, or at intermediate times, had, in addition, their separate meetings, and these generally preceding a Festival. To each of these classes of the congregation was allotted one Festival during the year, and a general Festival of the whole united "Choirs" took place annually. These subdivisions of the religious family might be termed the "Choir System;" and all exclusive meetings, or Festivals of the "Choirs," "Choir Meetings," or "Choir Festivals," denoting that the solemnity was appropriated to the particular "Choir" by whose name it was called.

To the outward observer of the Moravian picture, as presented to him for the first time, nothing appeared more striking than the white dress of the children, girls, and single Sisters. On their Festivals they were all seen thus attired, and the head-dress was the "Gemein Haube," or "Schneppel Haube," as it was sometimes familiarly termed, a cap worn by all the female portion of the congregation. It is now laid aside in America, but in Germany it is still preserved, and regarded with some degree of veneration by those who uphold, rigidly, the outward forms of Moravianism.

This cap is a singularly plain head-dress, generally consisting of four pieces or parts, and tied under the chin by ribbons of different colors, to distinguish the

"Choir." The children wore the light-red ribbon, the girls the dark-red, the single Sisters pink, the married women blue, and the widows white. By these simple badges the whole sisterhood designated its various "Choirs," and in the celebration of a Festival, the whole "Choir" appeared in its prescribed costume.

Previous to all annual Festivals and Sacraments, each "Choir" was wont to repair to its Principal, (Pfleger or Pflegerin,) the visit being usually performed singly by each individual, to receive admonition as to spiritual guidance and self-examination, which the approaching solemnities seemed to demand. The interview lasted about fifteen minutes, and the duties involved in it were regarded of serious import by all in whom an inner religious life was active. We may naturally suppose that this devotional regimen, in the earlier stages of Moravianism, was highly conducive to its advancement in true piety, and that such communings with a Superior were sought after and valued as precious moments; but as the community enlarged its limits, and the heart lost its purity, many repaired to the place of visitation with alloyed motives and feelings.

By many a spectator of the Moravian forms, these monthly "Speakings," as they were termed, were regarded in the light of the Roman Catholic confession, and the motives of that institution were imputed to the Moravian Sister, as she sat before her Principal. The interview, however, was of a somewhat different nature, as it consisted in a mutual interchange of Christian sentiment, without the exaction of any confession of past transactions. In such communings there may, naturally, have been acknowledgments of past error, on the part of the individual who called on his or her Principal, yet the design of this institution did not point to the confession, but rather to a perfectly unrestrained disclosure of Christian experience. The responsibilities of this office were held of no little importance, as the influence imparted by the person, either male or female, who dispensed the words of exhortation to each distinct "Choir," was supposed to keep alive the spirit of faith, hope, and love. The regular event of the monthly "Speaking" was the most appropriate precursor of the solemnity that was to follow, and had its chastening effect upon the soul of the candidate for the communion. Another precursor of these solemnities was the separate "Choir Meeting," which derived its beautiful and solemn feature from the exclusive number and distinct class of candidates for the Festival, and to which a peculiar tone of devotion was imparted in the forms of prayer and liturgic singing.

The origin of the Choir Festival generally attached itself to some bright point of history, where, in the past annals of the Church, a remarkable awakening had taken place in the earlier epochs of Herrnhut. Out of this origin some sacred feeling emanated, and, although the Festival was a matter of joy, the happiness of the day was always imbued with solemnity. On the opening of the Festival, in the morning, the event was announced from the belfry of the church by chorales, performed on wind instruments, and as the "Choir," in whose honor the day was celebrated, entered the hall of worship, these strains of solemn melody sounded impressively upon the ears of all. Within the precincts of the Sisters' House it was usual for the Sisters, on their own Festival, to receive the salutation of a choir of female voices, greeting them at daylight, before they rose, with anthems of joy. In addition to this, congratulations were extended to all those who were celebrating their anniversary, a custom whose derivation is traced to Herrnhut, where anniversaries are marked by affectionate congratulations on all sides. These were expressive of sympathy in the enjoyments of the "Choir," and when dispensed by the aged to the young, they were in token of a blessing upon their opening Christian career.

As to the services of the church during the Festival, they consisted in the usual forms of devotion, preaching and singing; the introduction and close, as well as that of the Love-Feast, always characterized by orchestral music, selected from the old and best masters of cathedral composition. This species of music received no small degree of cultivation; and, as it was expressive of the Moravian love of music in general, found a useful application in all solemn church celebrations. At an earlier period of

Moravian history, the Festival of the single Sisters was accompanied by a multitude of ceremonials and church services, yet these were so blended with vocal and instrumental music as to render the scene highly picturesque, viewed by a mere spectator, aside from its spiritual character.

In tracing the derivation of these rituals to their source, I must refer the reader to a remarkable Sisters' Festival, which took place in Herrnhaag, in the month of May, 1747. It has already been told that this place was the seat of the Brethren during the Count's exile, and that there was exhibited that excessive ferment which caused so much disfigurement to our early church. "Early in the morning," says the writer of the chronicle, who, from the language and terms, appears to have been a participant, "the Sisters were awakened from their slumbers by the voices of Anna[1] and the other Eldresses, greeting them in a well-known psalm. A second psalm followed, and upon hearing the third psalm, all arose and proceeded down stairs, singing together. At seven o'clock they repaired to the chapel, where the morning blessing was given by Papa.[2] After the usual morning services, the whole 'Choir' of maidens proceeded, at three o'clock in the afternoon, to meet the Sisters of Marienborn, three miles from Herrn-

[1] Anna Nitschmann, the chief Eldress of Herrnhaag, and previously of Herrnhut.

[2] Count Zinzendorf, who was thus familiarly called.

haag. They passed through the avenue leading in that direction, and when the two 'Choirs' came in view of each other, that of Herrnhaag divided, arranging itself on opposite sides, and permitted the procession from Marienborn to pass through. These were then greeted by Anna, she addressing Justina, Eldress of the Marienborn choir, and her colleague, Anna Johanna, addressing Salome, colleague of Justina. As they all moved in a body toward the church, the musicians,[1] who sat upon the oval bench before it, saluted them, and upon their entrance into the hall of worship, the trombones pealed forth sacred anthems, aided by the voices of the congregation.

"The whole number of virgins on this occasion was about two hundred and fifty, who were all, without exception, attired in white.

"Among the guests present were many of the families of the nobility. The hymn used for the Love-Feast was the Forty-fifth Psalm, the most appropriate cantata ever sung.

"Succeeding the Love-Feast, and after the interval of one hour, came the evening liturgy. Here the 'Choir' sat arranged as in the Love-Feast, and, during the meeting, the 'Te Sponsam' was sung. While this was performing, Anna Johanna arose, and, proceeding toward the Count and Countess, knelt before them, receiving their benediction, as

---

[1] Female performers.

well as that of Benigna, the Deaconess of the Single Sisters, and, at the same time, was ordained Eldress of the Single Sisterhood. Then all the Principals,[1] fifty in number, saluted her with a kiss, and the solemn scene drew tears from the eyes of every one present. The next meeting following upon this was the singing meeting, which was held in a most patriarchal manner by Christian."[2]

Our narrator informs us that the Illumination next followed, and that it was worthy of the occasion. The Sister's House was filled with light, and with various transparencies and inscriptions, all commemorative of the event. The Choir of Sisters went out by pairs, during the illumination, into the square before the house, and, while standing there, sung hymns of praise. After they had retired, and had closed their doors, the congregation sung before the dwelling "hymns of rest," (Schlaflieder.) Finally, between the hours of eleven and twelve o'clock, they closed the performances of the day by an evening blessing, dispensed by the Count, after which they all retired to rest, filled with the deepest emotions.

The Festival here described is illustrative of an over-wrought Moravianism that characterized the middle of the last century, and found its full de-

[1] Pflegerinnen, each having a small company of Sisters under her care.

[2] Christian Renatus, son of Count Zinzendorf. His portrait hangs in the church at Bethlehem.

velopment at Herrnhaag. Since then its tone and rituals have become greatly modified, and less obnoxious to the censure which, with some degree of justice, was cast upon it.

Up to a recent date, the Sisters' Festival was sustained in our villages with all its unique observances. The early salutation at the doors of the sleeping apartments; the procession to and from the place of worship, of girls in white apparel, with the characteristic head-dress and pink ribbon, and the whole of the front seats of the church presenting a uniform picture of the maiden's choir; the absorbing music of the orchestra; the promenades in the open air in the garden, with music in the intervals from an amateur company of musicians; the chorales on the trombones on the opening of the Love-Feast, as in the days of Marienborn and Herrnhaag; the congratulations extended by the old to the young, indicating their wishes for happiness now and solicitude for a life's peace in future,—all these demonstrations of a refined, cultivated, and deeply-devoted Christian life, were witnessed in our Moravian villages.

The Festival of the Single Brethren, too, had its marked features, and they passed through many of the solemnities that honored the Single Sisters, such as anthems and chorales on wind instruments in the morning, the harbinger of the Festival, the procession into the church, the enjoyment of Love-Feast and collations during the day, the final close at evening with some beautiful and stirring performance of the orchestra, introductory to the liturgy,—all these festivities constituted the round of a Christian Moravian's life, and lent to the aspect of his creed the realization of a heaven on this side of eternity.

We might term the Festival the great embodiment of the strongest characteristics of Moravianism, a perfect blending of profound religion with earthly pleasure. It is not often that we discover such a phenomenon in the social world that admits and exercises Christianity. There is a feeling of stern duty in its religion that too often blunts the pleasure of ordinary life, and the line drawn between the two is so strongly marked that one must be sacrificed to the other.

The spirit of the species of devotion shadowed forth in the sketch I have just given was of German extraction, and sprung from the national modes of life and thought of a people in whom a deep-seated feeling of religion is prominent. As long as the German element prevailed in our villages, and remained free from the influence of American enterprise and its materialistic tendencies, the pure scenes of the Festival were enacted in the manner drawn in the preceding picture. But time, which changes all things, is fast resolving the poetic into the commonplace, and as religion assumes the garb of austerity and stern conventionality, its spirituality becomes more dimly seen. To secure the influences of devotion upon the human mind, no scenes are better calculated than those springing out of the naïve and simple. In the attempts of art to present the most engaging pictures of humanity, or to portray such scenes as are of the most pure and spiritual tone, it should seek out nature, or man in such positions as conform most nearly to nature. In the outpourings of the soul, as we see them in the past history of the Moravian, in the unaffected and innocent manifestations of his devotional career, we are made conscious of a poetic, and even romantic blending of religious emotion with the every-day transactions of his social existence. To infuse into this existence the joys of religion, to make every spiritual motive identical with pleasure, the pleasure of the soul, was the great end of the Moravian Cultus. Any mode of worship that can clothe the Christian's faith in such enticing colors, or impart to the daily routine of a selfish and disappointed existence the sacred recreations that characterized old Moravian life, must serve to nourish the flame of religious thought, and keep pure and flowing the fountains of a simple but holy creed.

Yet in examining the question, why the Moravian Cultus produced such marked results upon the outward character and inner life of the individual, we cannot allow the influences exerted by music to escape our attention. As music constitutes the entrance to the world of spiritual thought, its study and practice tell, with remarkable force, upon the emotional part of the Christian character. From the earliest period in the history of the Brethren, its cultivation was an essential portion of all the rituals of the Church, and it not only proved the inspiring, elevating, and chastening handmaid of devotion, but gave vitality to all the forms of social life.

Although the idea of the Festival, in its application to religious purposes, is foreign to American thought, and forms no feature in our plan of worship, it is common in Europe; and where Roman Catholicism reigns, the festal holiday is a frequent occurrence. In those old countries it belongs to the traditions of the people, and on the days set apart for the celebration of those saints' anniversaries, which fill the Roman calendar, crowds are seen, in best attire, attending the cathedrals. Should it fall entirely into decadence here, we must attribute the misfortune, as we ought to deem it, to the great uniformity of American thought and feelings, on all points of custom, usage, and recreation. What is deemed admissible in Europe, where the force of tradition allows nothing to be lopped away, would be thought out of place here.

An old and beautiful custom prevailed in many households, and may still be found here and there to this day, of asking a blessing at every meal, in a hymn, consisting of a single verse. The verse, if sung at the breakfast-table, is accompanied by the reading of the Daily Text, a small manual, published annually, and containing texts from the Old and

New Testament, for every day, each text being coupled with a verse. In the memoirs of Zinzendorf and Spangenberg, reference has been made to the use of the Text-Book, and though it is no longer in as general use, as a pocket-companion, as it was in earlier times, yet it is generally adhered to by all staunch Moravians, and its perusal at the breakfast-table is a fixed custom.

Another favorite companion of the morning meal was the Birth-Day Book. In this repository were recorded the names of all friends, far and near, living and dead, the places of their nativity, birth, age, etc., making a record of those most dear to the heads of the family; and while the anniversary of their births is referred to, they are kept alive in the memory of cotemporary or surviving love and affection. As the Birth-Day Book acquired a somewhat venerable character in the family, as it passed down to posterity, the accumulation of names of former days gave it additional interest and value, and where it succeeded in escaping the wear and tear of time, and had outlived many generations, it was clung to as one of the relics deemed most worthy of preservation.

When traveling, the Moravian of the patriarchal times had his "Reiselieder," or traveling hymns. These, sung in the solitude of the chamber, before retiring, or at rising in the morning, or performed in agreeable chorus by several pilgrims, added solace to the journey, and, if on the mission of evangelical labor, assuaged its toils and hardships. We might raise up before us many a pleasant picture, if we were to imagine the traveling missionary, before starting on the errand of Christian love, pour forth in the depth of the forest those inimitable hymns we possess, and which, with the melodies that accompany them, remain intact. In addition to these, there were "Wiege Lieder," or cradle hymns, in which Christ, under the personification of an infant, is introduced, and made the subject of song for the cradled child.

As labor was placed in the same attitude it enjoyed in Herrnhut, as an active element of an ideal congregation, and carried out in reality by the followers of Zinzendorf, it requires notice, under the general head of a Moravian Cultus. In the earlier portion of our history in America, and even up to a very late period, labor had its dignity and its religious aspect, all of which it derived from the organization of social life in Herrnhut, of which ours was an imitation. The whole daily transaction of a commonplace life being imbued with one thought, which was always uppermost, and Christ being the embodiment of that thought, every human purpose became dedicated to it. Under this conception of the true end and aim of labor, no one considered it disgraceful to be engaged in pursuits of domestic economy, in trade or agriculture. To carry out the conception of Herrnhut, every calling had its solemnization. The reapers, the mowers, the ploughers, the washers, the scourers, had their Love-Feasts, and their appropriate hymns. When the reapers entered upon the harvest, or the ploughers commenced or ended their work, a Love-Feast opened the undertaking, or crowned its successful issue.

The "Spinne Lieder," or spinning hymns, were very common, and adapted to the exercises of that once useful art. We have still left recorded many amusing little morceaux, characteristic of the simple scenes that were enacted, when a company of Sisters sat with distaff or spinning-wheel, and whiled away the hours, with the accompaniment of hymns. Thus every day and every pursuit had its appropriate sacred lyric, sanctifying, beautifying, and ennobling life, and strewing its thorny paths with the roses of celestial hopes.

I recur to these observances of the fading past with peculiar emotions, as they are the indications of a poetical age, where the pictures of life have reality for their pencil, and the moral they inculcate sinks deeply into the heart of the living age. That faith, on which those early Moravian pilgrims grounded their hopes, was a sterling faith, undisturbed by the agitations of modern thought and investigation, and the hymns they poured forth under all the circumstances of rest, labor, and travel, were pure inspirations, and carried with them the beatitude of heavenly peace.

I have remarked that music characterized the whole life of the Moravian, in the sanctuary, in the family, in traveling, and at labor. Hymns were not only adapted to departure and rest, but were often sung by the Sisters when going from place to place; and it is related that those of Marienborn and Herrnhaag, while passing to and fro, used to make the woods resound with their chants. This music was, and yet is, of a high and classic order, being of the old German school, while the orchestral performances are chosen from the works of Haydn, Beethoven, Mozart, and others.[1] The Love-Feasts are generally enlivened with at least one passage from the Creation, the Psalms being printed and circulated among the congregation. Most of the quaint phraseology of the Moravian hymns has been expunged, and in addition to the numerous translations from the German, many of Watts's compositions have been introduced.

---

[1] Among those who first promoted and gave form to the Moravian Church music, may be named Tobias Frederick, a peasant boy, who appeared among the early emigrants of 1722, and was distinguished at the youthful age of thirteen years for his extraordinary musical abilities. He attracted the attention of the musical public in general for his genius; traveled through Denmark and Sweden, where, as well as at the University of Jena, he performed great services in aiding the work and knowledge of the Brethren, at that early period. He was appointed to the directorship of their sacred music at Herrnhut, in which capacity he raised its character to that standard of purity and harmony, in all its combinations, which render its approach to the ideal of an angelic choir as near as can be conceived. Tobias Frederick died in 1736, and, taken all in all, has never yet been equaled. (See *Croeger's Brüdergeschichte.*)

The German Hymn-Book contains the productions of older writers, from the middle of the seventeenth up to the end of the last century, and some even date as early as the latter part of the sixteenth century. Those authors whose lyrics are most copiously selected are Zinzendorf, his son, Christian Renatus, Anna Nitschmann, Luise von Hayn, Erdmuth Dorothea von Zinzendorf, Spangenberg, etc.; and among the older writers are found Paul Gerhard of the seventeenth century, Schindler, Heerman, Schütz; and still earlier, Luther and those of his time.[1] Of these bards, many be-

---

[1] The hymn-books now in general use in the Moravian Church are but concise abridgments of the older manuals of the Brethren. In reviewing the lyrical history of the universal Protestant Church, we are struck with the great productiveness of the early ages in sacred song. It is supposed that not less than 70,000 hymns are in existence, under the various forms of composition in which they have appeared from time to time. Of our primitive hymn-books, which were generally stored with the poetry of previous editions, the largest was that compiled in London by Zinzendorf in the year 1753, containing 2169 hymns, to which a second volume was added in 1754, comprising 1096 additional ones. In this second volume are to be found a large number of the improvisate effusions of the Count, which were occasionally gathered as they proceeded from the lips of this prolific bard.

The first form seen in this collection is that elementary species of the church hymn, which consisted of the Bible songs of praise, thanksgiving, and devotion, found in the various books of the Old Testament, from Genesis to Isaiah, and in the New Testament, from Matthew to Revelations. This was an ancient form of sacred psalmody, and common to the whole Christian Church in the remotest times of which we

longed to noble families, and we find the names of counts and countesses appended to a large portion

have any knowledge. These hymns are numbered from 1 to 110. We then find the Bible texts, from 111 to 193, arranged in verse, some of which may be classed among the most beautiful of all our hymns, such as the Twenty-third Psalm, rendered in German. These parodies were not confined to the Old Testament, but the texts of the New Testament are metrically arranged in the same manner as those of the Old Testament. The hymns numbered from 194 to 265 are translations from the Greek of the Eastern Church, from the Chaldaic of the Alexandrian Church, and from the Latin of the Western Church.

After these follow those properly termed the Hymns of the Ancient Brethren, Nos. 266 to 432, where the productions of John Hus,[1] of the fifteenth century, and Michael Weissen, of the sixteenth century, are brought to notice.

Then follow the hymns after the Reformation, such as the Augsburg Confession in metre, the symbolical hymn of Berne, the hymns of Luther, Speratus, Matthesius, N. Herrmann, etc., Nos. 433 to 509.

Nos. 510 to 821 comprise the lyrics of Nicolaus, Herberger, Paul Gerhard, Angelus, Heerman, and others; and the remaining hymns, up to 2169, are the compositions of writers who lived during the succeeding interval between this and the middle of the last century, soon after which there seems to have been a decline in this species of poesy, as few authors are recognized of more recent date than the year of Zinzendorf's death, which was 1760.

The most hallowed specimen of the quite ancient music still in vogue in the Brethren's Church, is the "Te Deum Laudamus," the composition of which is ascribed to Ambrosius, Bishop of Milan. This venerable production is now

1 The authority for this corrected spelling of the name of the Great Reformer, is Rev. Dr. Bomberger's edition of Hertzog's Cyclopedia of Biblical Literature.

of our German hymns. One of the most beautiful and simple of all is that written by Ludomilla,

---

nearly 1500 years old, and has been in general use throughout the Catholic and Protestant Churches since its first emanation from the church which gave it birth.

In connection with its origin, it is related of this hymn that when St. Augustine was converted to Christianity, and was baptized by Ambrosius, they sung the whole of the "Te Deum Laudamus" together, in alternate verses; Ambrosius began and Augustine followed, each composing a verse under the inspiration of the moment, the lines of which were afterwards preserved and handed down to succeeding ages.

Of the class of hymnologists enumerated in the sixteenth and seventeenth centuries, none was more fertile than Paul Gerhard, who was pastor in Berlin, and, subsequently, in Lubden, in Lower Lusatia. He was born in 1616, and died in 1676. The number of his productions, which were mostly sacred, was not less than 120, and far exceeded that of Luther's hymns, who wrote but 37. Of all the lyrical writers of his time, he was best acquainted with the wants and taste of the people, and more than any other wrote in the vein of popular feeling.

Nicholas Herrmann, the Cantor of Joachimsthal, is noted for many national hymns, the most celebrated of which is, "When my hour draweth nigh," "Wenn mein Stündlein vorhanden ist," etc.

Zinzendorf himself was so addicted to versification, that he not only extemporized, wrote, thought, prayed, and sung the exhaustless sacred themes that engrossed his soul, but engaged any one else in the exercise of poesy, wherever any latent talent for this gift seemed to dwell.

In the infancy of Herrnhut it was a universal propensity among its people to combine sacred song with all their aspirations, and when the Count found a peasant girl, or a peasant,

Countess of Schwarzburg-Rudolstadt, who died in 1672.

Einer ist es dem ich lebe,
  Den ich liebe früh und spät,
Jesus ist es dem ich gebe
  Was er mir gegeben hat.
Bin ich in sein Verdienst verhüllt?
Führe mich, Herr, wie du willt.

One there is for whom I live,
  Constant love to Him I owe;
All I have to Him I give,
  All I have did He bestow.
Am I in thy service still?
Lord, conform me to thy will.

---

inclined to metrical thought, he endeavored to bring forth some crude poetical effort. He was in the habit of assembling small companies, and proposing to them some subject, on which they all wrote, and then handed in their compositions for revision. He was particularly desirous of eliciting rehearsals from those Brethren who had encountered trials and severe mental vicissitudes in their journeyings, at sea, in prison, or among the heathen,—making them available as the choicest material for sacred song.

Singing is not merely a peculiarity of the modern Moravian, but was cultivated by the Unitas Fratrum and the Bohemian Brethren long before them, for we even find it among the charges brought against John Hus and Hieronymus of Prague, that they had made attempts to seduce the people over to their doctrines, by conveying these in sacred verse, and in the vernacular language!

The famous David Chystraeus, who delivered a discourse in 1569, on the state of the Christian churches in Greece, Asia, and Bohemia, testifies to this peculiar quality of the old Bohemian worship, and says that in all their meetings, the Brethren sung very delightfully.

The melodies founded on the rules of pure harmony, and emanating, as I have said, from the older schools of classic music, are distinguished for the soul that animates them, their depth and sincerity of thought. In most instances, they are sung with organ accompaniment, but it frequently occurs that they are heard with a full chorus of voices, without accompaniment, which gives them a striking and an abiding effect. Though not calculated for display, or to seize upon the popular or uneducated mind, they live forever in such hearts as have a genuine susceptibility for harmony, and have had this awakened by culture.

In Germany, the cultivation of music is closely interwoven with all the pursuits of life, and as long as it remains so essentially natural among our Moravian Brethren there, the ritual, in all its primitive forms, will be able to retain a foothoold. In this country, however, the musical tone and taste of our Moravian villages seem approaching their decadence, and, as a necessary result, the externality of devotion changes its whole character. The cause of this declension of music among us may be traced to that national pursuit of wealth, which debases all that is pure within, and leads the thoughts to all that is gross and glittering without.

The earlier history of the Moravian was the universal history of the human heart in the fervor of its youthful ebullitions. But when the primitive hymns of their first love had been culled of their extravagance, when the religious exercises became less numerous and more befitting the commonplace obligations of the individual, the tenor of Moravian life corresponded more nearly with the ideal of a perfect Christianity. Among the most engaging pictures to which the musical ritual gave rise, we must not overlook the funeral ceremony. In the village, every death is announced by a dirge on the trombones, mostly from the belfry of the church. The dirge thus played is selected with reference to the sex of the deceased, each having its appropriate death-melody. No soul escapes from its tenement of clay without this public signal to all the denizens of the village, and as those stirring notes ascend upward and vibrate around you, penetrating into every habitation of the living, the thoughts turn from the engagements of time, and dwell for the moment among the images of another world.

Most frequently these announcements come floating upon the morning air, as Death is a frequent visitor during night-time, or, should the event be in afternoon, the long-drawn notes of the trombone sound mournfully through the quiet evening. At such a moment, man feels oppressed with the cares of the day, and as he listens to this expressive and subduing language of tone, he feels the more deeply the force of the event which has just consigned another fellow-mortal to eternity.

The ritual commences even before the departure of the spirit, and as it begins to yield up its last earthly attachments and recognitions, a small circle may often be seen gathered around the couch, administering the offices of love in imparting the last blessing. This is usually performed when all expectations of a prolonged life are surrendered, and the candidate for the coming change is prepared to depart. Then the well-known hymn is not unfrequently sung:—

"Lord, let thy blest angelic bands
Convey my soul into Thy hands,
When soul and body sever;
My body, though reduced to dust,
Thou wilt, O Lord, I firmly trust,
Raise up to live forever.
Then shall I see Thee face to face,
In everlasting joy and peace,
And sing with all the saints above
The wonders of redeeming love.
O Christ, my Lord, I'll Thee adore,
Here and above for evermore."

Frequently the last blessing precedes death by several days, and long before the final flickerings of life are observed. In those instances the hymns of comfort and solace are repeated by the groups assembled around the invalid, if prompted to do so; but it is an invariable custom to sing verses, and frequently to administer the Sacrament, previous to his dissolution. The remains are usually placed the next day within the "Corpse-house," whither the friends of the deceased repair to gaze upon the face before its final disappearance from earth. A simple rose, the tribute from the hands of affection, is sometimes added to the lifeless figure, now attired in the white habiliments of the tomb. This ornament to the garb of death is expressive of peace and joy to the soul of the departed. In this silent sanctuary the little lamp is placed, and it is the office of some quiet and fearless Sister to repair there during the night to trim the beacon that custom deems needful for the lifeless body, while still within the precincts of the living. To many, this mission of the night would seem a fearful one, but to some there is a companionship in the cold form, the well-known lineaments addressing you, as it were, "Fear not! for while my body sleeps the sleep of death, my spirit reigns over and guards you."

In the church service, preceding the burial rites, the discourse not unfrequently bears reference to the deceased, and ends with a short memoir, either drawn up as an autobiography, or by the hands of some friend, giving the outlines of a past career, and expressive of its inner history. Some of the best vocal dirges are then sung by the choir, preparing the mind for the scene that is to follow. After passing from the church, the whole assemblage arrange themselves before the "Corpse-house," where verses are again sung, chorales played on trombones, and then the procession moves forward with solemn pace to the cemetery, the trombones preceding it, and playing the thrilling and harmonious music of the funereal ritual. Around the grave a similar scene is enacted, the voices of the multitude mingling with the notes of the instruments, played by four performers, who adapt the chorale to the subject of the occasion.

In Herrnhut, the burial rite, to which the early part of the evening is appropriated, is distinguished by a much larger number of instruments, ten performers often preceding the long train that winds its way from the church through the avenue of lindens to the "Hutberg." Many of these dirges are perfect compositions, and are finely invested with the solemnities of death, so that they have become consecrated to this sole event, and, when heard, bring up its associations in all times and places.

The same may be said of most of the other melodies of the Moravian repertoire. They become identified with the subject to which they are applied, and when heard by those who have learned and known them from childhood, bring up scenes of fond recognition. Thus the dirge of death and the song of triumph, the anthem of praise, the hymn of joy, are alike, in turn, appropriated to these successive events as they follow in the cycle of the Moravian year, and there seems to be a spiritual sustenance wanting when the pleasures of a musical Cultus are cut off.

It is among the striking attributes of a Moravian creed to surround the circumstances of death with the garlands and roses of a cheerful hope. Hence the cemetery, in many of our larger villages, following the design of the "Hutberg," becomes a cheerful resort; and while the bodies of the departed sleep beneath the turf, adorned with smiling flowers, expressive of heaven and typical of its realized joys, the living footsteps are seen to pace the walks around the grave, with thoughts chastened by the sacred spot.

On the celebration of the Birth-day, which is an obligation of no small import, the members of a family make their offerings in the shape of a table decked with flowers and small contributions, demonstrative of family loves; and, in many instances, hymns of congratulation are sung, to greet the recipient of the Birth-day.

In the ceremony of marriage, the older customs prescribed a Betrothal, a ceremony of serious and solemn accompaniment, in which the officiating clergyman delivered a feeling and impressive charge to the bridal pair, seated in the circle of numerous chosen friends. The scene was then cheered by wine and cakes, and closed by lively conversation. In the public ceremony of marriage, which followed a week afterwards, the rites were gladdened by a general Love-Feast, dispensed to the whole assemblage in the church where it took place.

Of all the religious observances, that of the Love-Feast is, perhaps, the most characteristic of the whole Moravian Cultus; and though I have frequently adverted to this custom, some further remarks seem necessary to illustrate the purposes of that institution. The rite itself was in imitation of the "Agapæ" of the early Christians, and was introduced at Herrnhut in the year 1727.[1]

---

[1] The "Agapæ" have had their origin traced to the apostolic times, and reference is made to them by Ignatius, in his Letters, Clemens, of Alexandria, Chrysostomus, in his Homilies, Hieronymus, Œcumenius, Theophylactus, and Theodoretus.

In those early ages the "Agapæ" were held prior to the Sacrament, with the view of showing the distinction between the two rites, and, at the same time, to furnish an imitation of our Saviour's last supper with his Disciples, before instituting the Communion itself.

Reference is made to these Love-Feasts in The Acts and in Paul's Epistle to the Corinthians, as well as in the reports furnished by Pliny to the Emperor Trajan, who there speaks of the Love-Feasts of the Christians.

Tertullian states that the aim of these Love-Feasts was the maintenance of brotherly love; that they were not intended to encourage much eating or drinking, but were dedicated to sacred singing and discourses.

In the "Concilio Gangrensi," a canon appears, which lays an anathema on all those who despise the "Agapæ!"

In primitive times the Love-Feast was accompanied by the "Kiss of Peace," a custom of an apostolic derivation as well as the ordinance itself, as found in Paul's Epistles, and many other writers. It was called the "Osculum Pacis," or "Sanctum Osculum," and was taken from the words, "Salute one another with a holy kiss." The Kiss of Peace was adopted in the Communion and in some of the Liturgies, but it is no longer in general practice, having been recently discarded in many of our American congregations. (See *Lynar.*)

At that time Zinzendorf, after a church service, was wont to send around to small conclaves of the Brethren refreshments from his own kitchen, to enable them to pursue their meditations under an enlivenment of the heart.[1]

The Love-Feast is applied to the gloomy and the cheerful; it invests the most solemn occasions with the light of hope, and sanctifies the most joyous moments with the solemnities of religion. Hence it was the scope of the Zinzendorfian worship to make the Christian life a constant reaction of parts, one tempering and influencing the other. The Love-Feast was thus appropriated to the Christmas celebration, the Easter solemnities, the cheerful festival, and, on august occasions, even to close the funeral service. To see this rite represented in its true spirit, and thus receive a proper appreciation of its intents and influences, the observer of Moravian life must be led through its whole diary. He must study and analyze it in its contrasting parts, but, above all, he must be sufficiently cultivated in the higher gifts of music to explain to himself the true and abstract motives of what, to the prejudiced mind, appear childlike and frivolous. The world's history has shown that the outward demonstrations of religion are displayed in a thousand forms, and I have observed that the design of the Moravian was to

---

[1] Eine Erquickung des Herzens, "a refreshment of the heart."

surround nearly all these forms with pleasure such as the soul delights in.

During the Love-Feast collation, which is preceded by hymns sung by the whole congregation, anthems are performed by the orchestra and chorus. The Love-Feast was often held in honor of the reception of some distinguished visitor from abroad, as already alluded to in the life of Spangenberg. At the schools in the olden times it was held on Examination-days, in the Hall, when the pupils were arranged on a long, continuous bench, and partook of their coffee and cakes in common with the audience. With the obliteration of old practices, this has been thrown aside as superfluous, although the primitive rite would even now contribute its share in fastening the affections of many a susceptible pupil to this adopted home of his youth.

In these outlines of the customs of a people who have flourished one hundred and thirty-six years, we find an application of the essential spirit of Christianity to the whole business of life. In those purer times, that have now become a matter of record and study, no material interests could absorb the feelings of the Moravian, and in the flow of geniality and mirth on social occasions, the whole tone of thought was tempered and refined by an education such as I shall describe in the picture of schools and their system of inculcation.

In the species of Christianity here developed, we have seen poetry called in aid to seize upon the affections, and by allowing the whole tenor of life to be dramatized, as it were, by all the exhibitions of a visible symbolism and the constant purification of soul which the language of sacred music must necessarily produce, it attained a degree of social purity such as history seldom presents.

VII.

CHRISTMAS CELEBRATIONS.

CHRISTMAS CELEBRATIONS have ever been pre-eminently marked by a festive character, and as this anniversary forms the opening of the great Christian drama, by bringing before the mind's eye the Saviour's nativity, it may be deemed the most appropriate introduction to the Moravian Festivals.

Throughout the Christian world the childlike pleasures of this sacred season endear it to the memory, and as the events of the Nativity lie open to the understanding and affections of the young, by the representation of a Divine incarnation in the infantile form, many of the religious performances have special reference to the wants and imagination of youth. Throughout our Moravian villages, the eve of Christmas is ushered in by a church scene, where appropriate decorations are frequently added, to enhance and enliven its interest. During the night when this fondly-anticipated ceremony comes off, a large portion of the surrounding rural population flock thither to witness it; to gaze at the paraphernalia, listen to the music, and partake of the Love-Feast. This has been a time-honored custom, and has always presented a singular contrast between the staid devotion of the Moravian himself and the boisterous merriment of the yeomanry, who are generally allowed free access to all the Christmas and New-Year's solemnities. Within the chapel, however, the utmost order and quiet are observed, and no molestation is offered to mar the designs of the Festival. It is not unusual to open it with the reading of the second chapter of St. Luke, one of the most poetical records of Holy Writ, where the memorable passage is introduced:—

"And there were in the same country shepherds abiding in the field, keeping watch over their flocks by night. And lo! the angel of the Lord came upon them, and the glory of the Lord shone round about them: and they were sore afraid. And the angel said unto them, Fear not: for, behold, I bring you good tidings of great joy, which shall be to all people. For unto you is born this day in the City of David a Saviour, which is Christ the Lord."

After this simple recital, a short discourse follows, and the musical rites open with an anthem, performed by full chorus and orchestra alternately, with the chorales of the whole congregration. The Love-Feast now approaches, consisting of cakes and coffee, and is distributed among all present, the congregation and guests forming, in some instances, a multitude of between one and two thousand.

During this collation a portion of Beethoven's Mass is performed, and the German words sung.

Sei willkommen,
Schöner Stern in heil'ger Nacht!
Ganz von Andacht hingenommen
Schau' ich deine stille Pracht!
Hosiana! Gelobet sey Der da kommt
Im Namen des Herrn, etc.

"Be thou welcome,
Beautiful star, in the holy night!
All transported by devotion
I behold thy quiet lustre!
Hosanna! Praised be
He who cometh," etc.

The singing on this, as on all liturgic occasions, is alternate between the male and the female, the youth and the adult portions of the worshipers, who, from time to time, are relieved by the choir.

In connection with the old Christmas-eve rituals there still remains an ancient vestige of the dramatic, savoring somewhat of the practices of the Church of Rome, yet so endearing by its simplicity and its strong affinity to those childlike interpretations of Christianity, on which the heart delights to dwell, that the colder age of new things has not yet been able to obliterate it. I allude to the introduction of wax-tapers. When the choir sings, "Mache dich auf, es werde Licht! denn dein Licht kommt, und die Herrlichkeit des Herrn gehet auf über dir!"[1] large trays of lighted tapers are brought in from the

[1] Arise! it becomes light: for thy light cometh and the glory of the Lord ariseth!

eastern side of the chapel, carried through the assembly and distributed among the children. To the aged, this sudden light appears in its true typical import, and the poetical scene is not undervalued by those who can read the mysteries of religion. But among the juvenile portion every face becomes radiant with joy at the appearance of this expected effulgent emblem, owing more to the general excitement of the moment than to the inspiration which the symbol should produce. The rural guests especially are absorbed in the spectacle before them, and seem to observe with intense delight the brilliant display of hundreds of wax-lights, held before the smiling faces of the children. The tapers are extinguished in gradual succession, the mugs are gathered and carried away, the music wanes, and the last tones of the organ fall upon the ears of the retiring multitude as they emerge into the frigid atmosphere of a December night.

This is the outline of the church ceremonial and of the scenes at the altar, at the opening of the Christmas week, and the description applies to our smaller villages even at this time; but as a more mixed population creeps into them, the simpler rites will gradually be exchanged for others, more in accordance with the wants of a new order of society.

Throughout the homes of the village, other scenes of like tendency are enacted. During the whole of the preceding week, the young men may be seen upon the bleak hills, where the moss is yet verdant and the hemlock and laurel are always cheerful, and grow luxuriantly in places where naught else will thrive, gathering huge piles and heaping on wagons those well-known Christmas-greens. The hemlock, sending forth its grateful aroma, is at any time a pleasant ornament, but when it comes in mid-winter to cheer us amid the general dearth of vegetable nature, we find it a most welcome emblem of festive happiness. The Moravian houses of the olden time were always redolent with this lively evergreen at the Christmas season, and its delightful perfumes bear along with them the associations of old memories. The evergreen and the hemlock-garland, interwoven with the glossy leaves of the laurel, or the bouquet of chaste flowers, are a constant feature of the Moravian anniversary of almost every description; and whether it be a Birth-day, a Christmas-tide rejoicing, a musical, a centennial, or a "Choir" festival, this green-leaved type of happiness greets the eye, and tells of the return of the wished-for day, which at its appointed time the heart sighs after. Long evenings are spent in weaving the wreaths, preparing inscriptions and transparencies, in harmony with the glad occasion. Each habitation, in which childhood constitutes a portion of the fire-side group, contributes its share to these displays of sacred art, and a succession of visitors is seen passing from door to door, to examine and discuss the merits of the "Decoration."

As you leave the chilly atmosphere of the ice-clad

street, and enter the comfortable domicile, where the green and aromatic drapery assails you, the design of the picture, being conceived in the utmost simplicity, breathing purity and sanctity of purpose, and elevating the imagination of the beholder to a world of sacred light, its true effects never fail being realized. Inscriptions referring to the Nativity are usually placed in the back-ground of the picture, which is illuminated in the evening, and to which are added figures and pictures illustrative of the Christian subject. A large portion of the room is sometimes occupied with the Christmas exhibition, and incongruous elements are occasionally brought into play, to please the young folks and the public, and to allow full scope to the ingenuity of the designer, who in most cases is the Pater Familias.

But when the "Decoration" is made to present a chaste adornment of wreaths, surrounding and overhanging the manger, with transparencies depicting the eventful night, as the artist's fancy may conceive it to have been in Judea—the Magi bearing spices, the star in the East—then it seems truly to fulfill its real design, and to come up to the ideal of a Christmas-eve representation.

During the whole of this week, the wax-candles—yellow, red and blue—and the coiled taper become important articles of merchandise, the demand for which seems unlimited. In former times these little accompaniments of the joyous season were productions of the Sisters' Houses, and many an aged

Sister made ample preparations to supply a round of customers.

In these dramatic conceptions of a sacred event, the heart, speaking of the past, seemed to grow apace, and the truly spiritual designs of all such visible representations have never been lost upon the juvenile portion of the household. These festivities, it is true, are purely idylic; they belong to an age where wealth and its train of influences have no overweening tendencies, where the mind has ample scope for its own quiet cultivation, and can rear itself within the isolation of unmolested thoughtful hours.

The whole Moravian Christmas-eve, as seen in one of our villages, was a truly beautiful and poetical picture. To strengthen this picture, however, we must always give it its rural associations, where the simplicity of an unadorned life, the freedom from conventionality, prevail, and where for the enjoyment of natüre's better privileges the soulless forms of society are excluded.

Christmas, and its train of pleasures, form but a portion of the festival season. The whole week intervening between it and New-Year is a continuation of the scene begun at the eve, as witnessed in the church and in the homes of the village, and the wings of youthful enjoyment continue their flight until New-Year's day has closed. The church solemnities of New-Year's eve are not less in importance than those of Christmas-eve, and are sustained till past the midnight hour, after the clock is heard to chime in the first day of the year.

It may deserve notice in this place that, in all the Moravian village congregations, diaries are kept of the most important events transpiring daily or weekly within their little circles throughout the year. In former times, the most trivial circumstances were recorded by the "Pastor Loci," in these registers, which were deposited in the archives of the church. During the exercises of New-Year's eve, a synopsis of the past year's diary is read, to which is added a list of the members, all the new accessions and departures, births, deaths, and marriages. The first of these meetings takes place at nine o'clock, and the second, or close, at eleven, which concludes with the opening of the New-Year. To perform this ceremony, the trombones are called in aid, and their loud peal is made to burst upon the audience, just at the moment the first tone of the clock in the belfry is heard to announce the hour of twelve. The speaker is cut short in the middle of his sentence, laying down in some eloquent passage his most forcible arguments, and all is made to give way to the sudden arrival of the new-born year.

VIII.

EASTER CELEBRATION.

"And as he went, a very great multitude spread their garments in the way, and others cut down branches off the trees and strewed them in the way. And when he was come nigh, even now at the descent of the Mount of Olives, the whole multitude of his disciples began to rejoice and praise God with a loud voice for all the mighty works they had seen. And the multitudes that went before and that followed, cried, Hosannah to the Son of David, blessed is He, a King, that cometh in the name of the Lord."

WITH the above recital in the life of our Saviour, and the Acts of Sunday, as they are styled, commence the exercises of Passion Week. The beautiful anthem of Hosanna, from the Choir, accompanies the reading, and is a fine introduction to the performances of this poetico-dramatical week.

To those who are strangers to the duties of the sanctuary, the readings of Passion Week offer many fascinations, as they attract them to services which from first to last are filled with interest. The evening and day services of this week constitute some of the most interesting of the year, and are attended by full congregations, who are absorbed in the affecting narrative, as it proceeds onward through the vicissitudes of a Redeemer's life to the final sacrifice.

Under the Moravian forms, these readings are interspersed with numerous illustrations and embellishments of solemn melody, imparting additional pathos to the various scenes as they pass before the hearer, and enlist his feelings by an exhibition of the melancholy beauty of the divine picture presented to his view. The representation of the sacred drama, with the aid of poetry, melody, and an occasional appeal to the senses, in various minor ceremonies of church worship, has been one of its most cherished features.

In contrast with the joyous festivities of Christmas, its evergreen wreaths and picturesque adornments of hearth and altar, there is a sublime and plaintive coloring thrown over the whole Easter solemnity, which binds it fast to the affections. Here the glorious strains of the Christmas anthem are exchanged for the dirge-like hymn, which, when sung, as it frequently is, without organ accompaniment, by full-toned voices, and in judicious accordance, constitutes the most impressive vocal music. Every evening of the week, until Thursday, there follows a continuation of the sacred history, but on Maunday Thursday, Good Friday, and Saturday afternoon, the meetings are held during the day. On Maunday Thursday two readings precede the Sacrament. On Friday morning and afternoon some of the most solemn scenes of Holy Writ are passed in review, and every remarkable passage in the sufferings of Christ is accompanied by a suitable hymn sung during the intervals. In the evening the readings of the day are closed with the passage, "When the even was come, there came a rich man of Arimathea, a city of the Jews, named Joseph, an honorable counselor, and he was a good man and a just, and there came also Nicodemus, which at the first came to Jesus by night, and brought a mixture of myrrh and aloes, about an hundred pound weight. Then they took the body of Jesus, and wound it in linen cloths with the spices, as the manner of the Jews is to bury," etc. The whole of Good Friday's exercises are then closed by a Liturgy. This Liturgy is perhaps one of the finest church services we have, and the parts being alternated between the pastor, the joint congregation, male and female portions, and the choir, it relieves the common order of church singing of its monotony.

Generally, upon the quiet Saturday afternoon, or Great Sabbath, there is a moderate assemblage met together in Love-Feast. Its participants are supposed to enjoy the meal of love with each other over the grave of the Saviour, while He reposes in the tomb of Joseph of Arimathea, previous to the great event, on the succeeding morning. In Bethlehem, on the evening of the Great Sabbath, the exquisite performances by the choir, "Jesus bowed his head," etc., takes place. It is a composition requiring all the aid of musical proficiency to receive its due effect, and is never attempted in the smaller villages.

Very early in the morning, and long before dawn, it has been an old custom to go around the village and awaken the still sleeping inhabitants by an Easter morning chorale, performed on the trombones. This is one of those incidents of Easter which impart to its celebration its old and essentially Moravian feature, and, I trust, that the genius of innovation may not extinguish this exquisite poetry of the past, and allow the good people of the village to sleep into the Easter morning without this melodious announcement. Should this, like many other institutions, pass away, it is no idle hope, that some new generation coming after us may strive to reawaken the lost and simple spirit; that it may possibly throw off the *refinement* of these latter days, and go back to the naïve and the sincerely beautiful. This early announcement is, certainly, the finest conceivable opening of that eventful anniversary, and I would look upon its obliteration from the customs of Moravian life, like that of many others, as much to be deplored.

The early morning service is still retained, after which a procession to the graveyard takes place, always in time to meet the rising sun. Here the trombones perform their part with marked effect, and contribute not a little to the beauty of the ceremonial. When the Easter ceremonies are favored by an early spring, and the morning air is serene, the procession to the graveyard is replete with the finest emotions. We are now not merely reading the event, but are acting it over, under the inspiring influence of the open air, at break of day. The locality of the Nazareth Cemetery is peculiarly interesting, and for the opening of Easter morning, there can be no place more worthy of selection. At this early hour the scene around breathes the deepest tranquillity. Picturesque in all its parts, a perfect, and even faultless landscape sleeps before you at six o'clock of our Easter morning, with the eastern light swelling into the bright glow of sunrise. Then the impressive words of the Litany, and the outpouring of those harmonious themes, to which the trombones are so well adapted, summon up thoughts that are precious and enduring for the soul.[1]

---

[1] In connection with our Easter celebration, and all the observances of Passion Week, it may not be deemed inappropriate to refer to those early customs of the Roman Catholic Church, called Easter Plays, and recorded among its institutions of the fourteenth and fifteenth centuries. The crucifixion, interment, resurrection, and ascension of Christ, formed the subject of these sacred dramas, whose origin may be traced as far back as the twelfth century.

These "Easter or Passion Plays" were purely devotional in their aim, and seem, originally, to have consisted in mere recitation on Palm Sunday and Good Friday, by various persons, representing Christ, the Apostles, Herod, Pilate, etc., alternating with choral melody. Sometimes the parts were divided between the clergy, who, by turns, rehearsed the history or chaunted the words of Christ or those of the other characters in the sacred history, allowing the hearers to participate in a portion of the dialogue or narrative.

The resurrection was not unfrequently treated in the same manner. Three priests, representing the three women at the tomb, were seen at the holy sepulchre, erected for the purpose in the church, and addressed the angel sitting there, and after being apprised by him that Christ had arisen, they returned to the altar, and announced the tidings in an appropriate song, composed in honor of the event.

From these simple sacred rites the spiritual drama seems to have derived its origin, many of the accessories of a theatrical exhibition being subsequently introduced, to give effect and interest to the proceeding.

The locality for these performances, and in particular that of Good Friday, was the church, and they were mostly transacted at night; they were called "Ludus de Nocte Paschæ."

The worshipers were not satisfied with the representation of the Passion Week only, but went through the whole history of our Saviour, his birth, the appearance of the Magi, the life of the Virgin Mary, the illustration of the parables, and that of the wise and foolish virgins.

The language employed in these rehearsals was Latin, but after the laity were allowed to take part in them, the German was substituted, with occasional Latin passages introducing old hymns.

The object of these ancient dramatic performances was religious instruction and edification; they had in view the visible exhibition before the minds of the people of the great truths of their faith. The spectacle, in all its inner meanings, was deeply religious, and closely combined with the general church doctrine.

As many improprieties crept into these ceremonies, a decree was issued against them by Pope Gregory, and, instead of their being held within the church, they were removed into the open air, and the market-place was often the scene of the scriptural drama, after witnessing which the spectators withdrew into the church. At a later period their relations with church worship entirely ceased, and they became more secular in form and spirit.

These performances were largely attended, and became very popular in the several Christian countries of Europe, for, having originated in Germany, they were introduced into France, England, and Italy. As long as they preserved a connection with devotional service, they were found to answer a good purpose, by giving visibility to sacred history among a people who were deprived of education and all the modern facilities of reading Scripture; but as an application to secular pleasure followed the strictly dramatic church service, the performance itself passing out of the hands of the clergy, they no longer retained their religious character or exercised the influence that was shown in their original design. (*Neumaier's Christliche Kunst.*)

IX.

EDUCATION AND SCHOOLS.

In the early history of Herrnhut, the Brethren directed some of their first efforts to the subject of education. The grand mission of the Moravians was the great evangelical enterprise, and for the promotion of that end, education became an incidental measure. Originally, the clergy, missionaries, and those employed in the sacred and educational offices were not distinct from the rest of the community, but the tendency of education and social life was such as to render all capable of filling any of these offices.

A large institution for the special instruction and training of Brethren was established in the Wetterau, in 1739, under the superintendence of John Nitschmann, having a direct reference to the great work of the missions, but in this school they were not merely taught literary and religious knowledge, but were exercised in various departments of useful labor. The same principle was an inherent feature of Herrnhut life and training, and had in view the general exercise of bodily and mental powers, and the preparation of all alike for the future service of the church.

In this regard those primitive times knew of no distinction between laity and clergy.

At a later date regular institutions of learning sprung up, aiming at a more complete course of study, separating the theological pupils from those designed for the ordinary pursuits of life, and receiving a support from the public at large. This plan exists at the present day. Their chief field is in Germany; but in addition to the German schools, they extend over Switzerland, Holland, Ireland, England, and the United States; and in the course of little more than a century have, from the small beginning in the Wetterau, increased to the number of fifty. Both male and female pupils are admitted each into their allotted institutions, which are resorted to by all classes of society both in Europe and America. These schools are usually of moderate size, their number of inmates in Germany extending from fifty to one hundred. Our own institutions at Bethlehem and Salem are much larger, the number of girls exceeding one hundred and fifty in the former, and frequently two hundred and fifty in the latter, while at Litiz they seldom exceed one hundred. The boys' school at Nazareth has, for some years past, averaged about one hundred.

Like Moravianism itself, these schools have never been characterized by that overweening popularity which seizes upon the admiration and meets with the approval of the great and indiscriminate public, and grows rapidly into favor, in order rapidly to lose it again. They have made their appearance in different localities, where the Moravians had their early settlements, and in no instance have they lost their hold upon public esteem.

In our European schools, the rule of limiting pupils to a moderate number works with marked success, and, among ourselves, it has been found to be a safer and more judicious course to train a small number well, than a large and promiscuous mass of youth imperfectly and superficially. But whether heart or mind engage the preceptor's efforts, a system of training must lay the basis of all instruction, and that training constitutes education in its intrinsic meaning, such as it has been the aim of the Moravian to impart. A systematic endeavor to train operates with less restraint on the pupil, and with more successful results on the part of the preceptor, in Europe than here. Man there being born to *order*, to a tamer submission to authority and a reverence for official dignity, in a degree unknown among our own people, the youth are more pliable, and education is more plastic. It is partly owing to this national characteristic of an unrestrained freedom of action, and a want of that which so strikingly characterizes the German,—a stern regard for order, that a three or four years' term becomes an essential condition to the success of a Moravian training.

A large portion of our American youth are justly amenable to the charge, that they never had serious or positive inculcations as to the great virtue of order. It has been the misfortune of many to have been taught that a reversal of this great European virtue would constitute a point of merit, and when such arrive at our schools, they find they have to start from the lowest step of the ladder. They find that brightness of intellect is, in some measure, a secondary affair, and that education, in its Moravian signification, expresses something more than mere intellectual cultivation; that its arena is not the literary tilting field, but that they must now be called upon to pass successful muster beneath a moral military discipline. The best lesson the youth of the republic could learn under this head, would be that which might be drawn from the training of the steed, which, let him be of the most perfect form, agile limbs, and purest blood, would be entirely valueless unless his noble instincts were curbed, moulded, and directed to some practical turn by his master, man.

But even American youth, with their peculiar bent for freedom, have, in the majority of instances, succumbed to the discipline of our schools, provided they have been placed there at an age of susceptibility and obedience, and have come with moral natures capable of being softened, even after they had been partially perverted by wrong guidance, or no guidance at all. The first year's apprenticeship these young disciples have to undergo is occupied in expelling the vicious qualities of a previous education, that had no fixed aim, nor tended toward any definite result; an education that had given unrestrained employment to the brain, but without reference to gradual development, or a wise limitation of studies.

To furnish the reader with an explanation of the merits of the system by illustration, I shall commence with the routine of one of our boys' schools.

Each of these schools stands under the direction of a Principal, who, in some instances, resides within the building itself with the pupils. The Principal and his wife are to be regarded in the light of parents of the large family, and are appealed to under all circumstances of a parental nature, or when long absence from home seem to form a vacant place in the hearts of children, which kindred ties alone can fill.

The division of the Institution into Rooms is one of its most striking peculiarities. In each of these we find two colleagues, or companion teachers, who live constantly with the pupils, taking watch over their charge by turn, and each serving his day in rotation. It is the duty of the Room-teacher to rise with his fifteen or eighteen boys, the largest number a Room should reach, to take them to meals, to morning prayer, and to remain with them, while pursuing their preparatory studies, until the eight o'clock bell announces the commencement of the school day. From that time the teacher is engaged in different departments, he himself teaching; the boys, who constitute his Room, are distributed throughout the different classes, higher or lower, according to their grade of merit and proficiency, without reference to their ages or the Room in which they live. At the hour of eleven the teacher of the Room takes them in charge till twelve o'clock, when the dinner bell summons all down to the dining-room.

In order to render this performance a creditable one, no little skill and some military tactics are required at the hands of the tutors. Dining, as also partaking of both the other meals, becomes a practice put into systematic form, and is a part of the great whole of the general pedagogic plan; and, indeed, if we consider how large a share of attention it occupies in the affairs of life, and how absorbing is the interest in all that relates to it, we may not wonder that it engrosses some attention, as a part of education. The going to and returning from the "Salle a manger," must be a quiet and regular proceeding; the teacher follows in the rear of the procession, and a Pythagorean silence is enjoined from the time of departure to the repast until it is accomplished.

So strict, in former times, was this Pythagorean doctrine, from which strictness, however, there has been a slight departure, that while at table the pupils were wont to indicate their wants by raising the hand, and designating the size of the bread, or proportion of meat, etc., by the number of fingers held up. This rule of perfect silence has had the best influence, and when strictly regarded at the dinner, affords one of the most admirable exercises in the whole daily routine. In the olden time the meals were always opened with a verse, which was sung by the united voices of the pupils; but of later times, singing, unfortnnately, has been exchanged for simple reading of the grace.

A custom was introduced at Nazareth Hall, and for some time preserved, of reading aloud during dinner by one of the pupils; but the general din of knives and forks, plates, and feet, caused many interruptions to the hearer, and rendered the history or story a work of fragments, only enjoyed at intervals. But reading, it has been found, is no proper adjunct of the repast, as the mind during that time requires anything but serious or reflective thought, and the digestive powers should be left to their undisturbed sway. The piano, however, would form a pleasant companion of the dining-room, and cheerful music would lend an increased charm to the gastronomic enjoyments of the pupils.

After the mid-day repast, of which the bill of fare, were it produced, would be very laconic, the family regulations proceed; the teacher taking his "Room" under his care until two o'clock P.M., when all once more disperse into their classes, which, having occupied three hours in the morning, require but two in the afternoon. At four, the time for recreation arrives. Then the teacher on duty again marshals his troop, and the woods are sought or a walk is had, which occupies the interval of daylight. On the play-ground there are many amusements to employ both teacher and pupil, and these are participated in together. The return to supper now follows, and this being dispatched, the evening is closed by "Preparation," or an hour's study, which, among the older pupils, extends to two hours, to enable them to duly qualify themselves for the succeeding day's exercises.

When the teacher retires with his pupils for the night, the solemnities of prayer are observed; he paces the dormitory until perfect quiet tells that all have gone to sleep, and then resigns his "Room" for the next day to his colleague, to go through the same process of watching, drilling, reproving, entertaining, and instructing in the elements of wisdom, a family of youth, who have all the waywardness, the caprice, and the innocence of childhood.

The scheme of academic life being on the plan of the family, the tutor is required to absorb all the affections of the "Room" over which he presides. In the intervals between school hours it becomes his duty to amuse his pupils; and in order to render his business a grateful task, and to lighten the burden resting upon him, he often seeks to regale the hours by stories, amusements, games, and reading. These avocations seem to render his own calling, in some measure, supportable, and to reconcile the unruly spirits placed under his guardianship, where they are deprived of the luxuries of home, to the restraints which a rigid system imposes upon them. But a long continuance of service such as this is apt to wear upon the preceptor and make inroads upon his health and happiness, and it is requiring too much of one and the same individual to exact of him more than five or six years of this species of tutorial life. In this space of time he will have outlived several generations of pupils, among whom a striking diversity of temper will have been encountered; while, on the part of their preceptor, the greatest trials of fidelity of purpose, warring with the weakness of humanity, are concomitants incidental to his calling. Two great interests are here always at work, and while the sympathies of the disinterested observer side, naturally, with the pupils, the greatest self-sacrifice is going on in the mind and physical energies of him who controls them.

Under the Moravian *regime*, however, the teacher's career is regarded in the light of a probation, and all his sacrifices of health and personal ease, and a long durance within the walls of a secluded boarding-school, are made subservient to the one great end of removing every selfish claim, and arriving at a more perfect fulfillment of Christian denial. The teacher's life itself in these institutions becomes a training, both as to habit and thought, and though accompanied with some disadvantages, by weaning him from society and debarring him from acquiring the tact and accomplishments of conventional life, yet the more lasting and important influences are left behind on mind and heart.

It has ever been deemed essential that the teacher be educated within the walls of the Moravian school, not only to capacitate him for its peculiar mode of inculcation, but, at the same time, to render him proof against the difficulties and trials of his pedagogic career. It appears to be a rather neglected, but most commendable usage, for the teacher to extend the pleasures of the family to his circle of pupils by that most admirable of all the relaxations of a vacation, a pedestrian tour. In this regard, the customs of the European schools deserve our attention and imitation. While corresponding in their general regulations very nearly with our own, the schools of Switzerland, and particularly those of Geneva, which stand deservedly among the best in Europe, are noted for Alpine tours made during the summer vacations, and extending across the Alps to Italy as far as Milan and Venice. These rovings among the mountains, with "Alpen-stock" and knapsack, often continue for several weeks, and in the school of Töpfer they have resulted in one of the most entertaining and admirable works, pleasantly and naïvely written, by Töpfer himself.[1]

[1] Voyages en Zigzag, ou Excursions d'un Pensionnat, en Vacances. A book copiously illustrated with Swiss scenery, amusing and grotesque school-boy tableaux, and fine delineations of nature and academic life. It has gone through numerous editions, and has received a deserved popularity.

The custom is not confined to the Swiss schools only, for we find some of the "Pensions" of Southern Germany sending out their lads, under a similar equipment, to rove through the mountains and sail on the lakes of Switzerland, and thus enjoy the sunny-side of a school-boy's life. The scheme is more practicable in a country where the youth are collected from different parts, and where a return home, during a four or five weeks' vacation, is precluded; but even in our own country, circumstances would often render the excursion feasible and desirable, and drive away the dullness of holidays spent within the solitary walls of the school. A ramble amid our own romantic and primeval woods would operate with good effect upon the practical and artistic susceptibilities of the pupil, and we should find a visible improvement among our own youth of either sex in the cultivation of a love of nature, grow out of such expeditions into the mountains, under the guidance of an instructor, whose fine tastes could give direction to the imagination of those under his or her charge.

It is not too late in the day nor too antiquated in purpose, even in these more prosaic times, to revive those earlier customs, and we may as well look to a revival of old forms of life to add to its excitements as to seek exploded and antiquated costumes to deck the outer man.

The whole gastronomic policy of our schools has been, and is yet, in some mitigated degree, under as wise a jurisdiction as the intellectual regimen prescribed to them. A diet that brings health to the system and roseate hues to the cheeks is, above every other, the true food of the body, and the wisdom of educational government lies in furnishing that exercise and pure air which are the chief promoters of hygiene. As to the nature of the exercise prescribed to the pupils, it consists mostly of a walk in the woods or into the surrounding country, and while at the play-ground, the game of ball is a frequent and favorite amusement.

Gymnastics have been introduced, wherein they are at liberty to test the strength of limb and practice in feats of agility. These may have a good end in view, so far as relates to the development of muscular powers; but the old custom of roving at large was always a pastime that filled up the vacant hours with the greatest zest, made nature a delightful companion, and refreshed the jaded mind by giving the limbs their free scope in the unrestrained amusements of the "Round Place."

I have said that the tutors themselves frequently share in the amusements of the green-wood, and rivalries at various games oftentimes spring up between themselves and the boys. Winter evenings call for mental recreation, previous to the hour of "Preparation," or that portion of the night which closes with study; and to those teachers gifted with the somewhat rare faculty which can invent a tale after the manner of the Troubadours, as it proceeds, it was, and is, a source of no little pleasure to find themselves surrounded with an audience of wondrous and gaping listeners, waiting in anxious suspense for a denouement which still lies hidden within the mazes of the story-teller's brain. Legends, after this fashion, are usually furnished by installments, and the evening's entertainment terminates with a "to be continued," and, as long as the narrator has the ingenuity to sustain the interest of his story, he can command that most desirable state of things in the "Room," a breathless silence.

In presenting these recollections of the past, as well as existing diversions of the Moravian Boarding-Schools, I am indicating the different points of a picture, of which the *tout-ensemble* has ever been pleasant and instructive to look upon. In the grown-up man or woman, whose memory recurs to the scenes I have touched upon, and who figured among them, emotions are awakened which are sacred to themselves, since the events on which they are based form an impressive point in their earlier lives.

Many of the youth themselves, participating in all the forms of a Moravian Cultus, witnessing our musical ceremonials, our poetical rites, enjoying our cheerful Love-Feasts, and sojourning long enough among us to go through a repetition of the Christian year of Moravian life and festivity, become imbued with ideas of the loveliness of Christianity which the world could neither "give nor take away." Under this combination of influences, the results of education are, in a large degree, purely *emotional*, and the moral character is more firmly moulded by heart-culture than by that of intellect.

The views I have taken of scholastic life are chiefly in reference to Nazareth Hall, and where they apply to the female character, to Bethlehem, Litiz, and Salem schools; but the spirit exhibited in them has been the invigorating element of all the Moravian institutions in Europe.

Having previously made use of the term *emotional education* as being one of the results of the Moravian system, I shall now add a few remarks on the meaning of the expression, before speaking of the intellectual department.

In the Moravian forms of life, the warmth of soul and geniality of social intercourse that spring from German nationality, are strikingly apparent. At the same time, we can trace much that partake of an emotional bias in the customs still reigning at Herrnhut. Among these we have the method of singing the hymns of the church, which all the children there learn so perfectly, that not even a book is used in service, and frequently, not a line read aloud by the pastor. The hymns are familiar to all, and can be caught up by every one as soon as he hears the first line started.

The custom of reciting the hymns was made a universal practice in the Moravian schools, and, although now no longer strictly adhered to in this country, was once a regular weekly exercise. By the Moravian youth a twofold object was gained—that of learning to sing the tunes of the church, and of becoming versed in the beautiful productions of our hymnology. All the pupils imbibing the spirit of these sacred verses, and acquiring the old German chorales at the same time, found themselves entering upon a province of instruction which I have termed emotional.

In America we still adhere to the practice of having weekly singing-schools, but less regard is paid to the cultivation of the chorale than formerly, and our music is, in some degree, tainted with the false taste of modern psalmody, too much in vogue in this country. The exercises in choral singing by whole classes is a feature of our system which cannot be too highly recommended; it has been introduced in many American schools, and, indeed, is an old custom among them, which, from time to time, has suffered neglect. It is the primary step to an emotional education, which, in connection with the intellectual department, should form the highest aim of the instructor of youth. By imbibing the first principles of harmony, such as the old Lutheran chorale exhibits, the foundation is laid for a good superstructure of musical thought, on which much of the refinement of human life is built. The subject of educational discipline is not converted into a mere thinking, calculating machine, but that mysterious portion of the organism termed the heart, is awakened into sympathetic action with the brain.

To these exercises in singing I must add the very essential portion of a Moravian cause of instruction, music on the piano, as conducive to the general results of the species of culture referred to. Whether the pupil makes much actual progress, or becomes a proficient in the art, is not the sole inquiry; the aim being more a general refinement of thought and introduction to musical feeling, produced by an acquaintance with the choicest airs and sonatas of Mozart, Haydn, and Beethoven, than to send forth accomplished musical scholars.

Lessons are given by those progressive steps from simple elements to higher composition that characterize the literary studies of our schools. Instruction in instrumental music thus forms a conspicuous feature, and in the female academies the success is more visible, in so far as relates to mere accomplishment; but in considering music as a medium of refinement, its influences are as fully manifested in our male as in our female schools. This whole process of education secures the affections of the youth, who become attached not only to the localities of his school-boy years, but to the forms of worship and the solemnities by which he is surrounded, and in this species of education fond reminiscences are sown for all his future life.

The strongest evidences of this fact are to be seen in the frequent revisits to the Moravian schools, by pupils who have grown up to manhood and venerable age, and also during the last few years, in the Reunions convened at Nazareth Hall, where some memorable and affecting scenes have been enacted on the part of the rejuvenated old men. Similar instances take place in the visits of aged ladies to the schools of Salem, Bethlehem, and Litiz, and the return to those old homes of their childhood always results in a declaration and outpouring of their affections for persons, localities, and early transactions in life, connected with that poesy of the heart, which never fades away, even when all else becomes callous.

In connection with these views, I may add that the plan of the family, though often attempted on a small scale, is not generally thought to be successful in its application to educational purposes; and if we consider the difficulties to be encountered by the principal and preceptor, in conciliating the conflicting wishes, and guiding the habits of a mixed community of boys, gathered from all opposite points, and reared in contrasting circumstances of life, we may infer how unelysian the joys of the family might be. But notwithstanding many warring elements are occasionally found to render the social life of our schools imperfect, the moral and intellectual regimen prescribed softens down many asperities, and renders the family plan a successful one.

In the long history of Moravian boarding-schools, instances of a happy realization of an ideal life could be pointed out, which the memory of the old man recalls with delight, and to which the venerable dame of the living times reverts with yearning emotion.

All these results are the characteristics of an emotional education, a growth in man's psychology, separate and distinct from that of the mere intellect, and having an immediate bearing on those grand aims and designs of life which make it a question of immortality. To these first developments of an inner life, made in our schools without any regard to creed, sect, or dogma, but brought forth by the cultivation of the simple Moravian hymn, with its unaffected Christianity, the pupil is often known to pay his acknowledgments at an after-period, when long intercourse with the world has proved that mere intellectual knowledge is wisdom under a soulless personification.

As regards the intellectual part of the system, it may be remarked that a large and captious programme has never been aimed at in our mode of instruction, the whole scheme being a development of mind by that gradual process which fits one stage of its growth for entering upon a successive one. To teach the youth *how* to learn, rather than to make him *learned*, was ever and still is the object of Moravian instruction.

First in importance is the rule of *writing* all lessons committed to memory. This limits the amount of learning, but conduces to thoroughness and correctness, the basis of the whole mental superstructure. History is given in the form of a lecture. The reading of some chosen passages of the world's most eventful and striking periods occupies the hour, before a class of fifteen or twenty pupils. A synopsis or outline of the portion accomplished during that time is thus furnished by the tutor, which, being copied by all the class, learned, and digested, is recited at the next lecture. Formerly, nearly all branches of study were inculcated in this way, but as the labor of revising each task fell upon the teacher, it became too onerous, and the text-books of other schools of the country have been allowed in certain studies to supersede that old and unrivaled plan by which knowledge is left but slender means of escape from the youthful student. It is not only the interest awakened during the hour of school in the fate of empires, or the character of the hero, that comes within the lecturer's plan, but the very habit of writing down the outline and learning thoroughly all it embraces, renders the process of this species of instruction unsurpassed. It is not the aim to teach the pupil the world's whole history, and furnish the names of those who have figured therein, and the years whence they all date their origin, in order to send forth good historical scholars; but, rather, to select the auspicious epoch when some remarkable convulsion of human thought and action took place, casting on the surface of time beings of remarkable endowments, and concentrate the young mind's powers upon the contemplation of such scenes, in order to bring about the development aimed at by every true system of education.

The tendency of the mode of tuition now under review, is to render the habits of thought and action *correct.* This principle is nowhere better illustrated than in the careful and punctilious revision of tasks, which the pupil invariably submits to the tutor. By suffering no error to go unheeded, the mind of the scholar passes through an ordeal of discipline, which in after-life fixes the character, and leaves indelible traces behind. Indeed that cardinal point of *correctness* stamps the system as an unequaled one, and forms the secret of all early training.

In explaining geometry, ample opportunity is given for the exercise of the pupil's ingenuity and logical acumen, by the manner the teacher adopts of first exhibiting his demonstration on the black-board, and then putting the capacities of the class to the test, by allowing every member of it to try the solution himself.

It has long since been laid down that all heads are not adapted to all studies, and the grand result of every educational effort should tend to train the mind for the task of grasping the ends and aims of its own individuality. The scope of the mode of instruction we are considering seems calculated to achieve this purpose.

In order to mould the character into forms of correctness, and lead it in the walks of system and regularity, its whole scheme has been most profoundly studied, and all its details nicely weighed. To accomplish all this, however, a short term of pupilage is not adequate. The uncontrolled and neglected subject who comes here to be instructed in mind and guided in heart, cannot be led into the straight path before having gone across the rugged and craggy defiles of correction and severe discipline. To bring this about, sometimes requires a penance of years, but the process is in most cases successful, wearing off the rough surface of the diamond, and exhibiting the fair glittering qualities that lie within.

I have previously observed that the Moravian school makes but little parade of knowledge, and does not promise to lead the mind of the child through the whole domain of science. This is not promised, simply because it cannot be done; and it would be catering to an age of false pretensions, an age in which varnish, veneering, and glitter are worshiped, to hold out any visionary and superficial plans of instruction. The results of these literary pursuits are found more in the general progress of mind than in the attainment of any showy accomplishments.

The mental faculty trained and disciplined in the paths of science by the same laws it was two thousand years ago, eschewing every new process of advancement, and avoiding every open and precipitous path into the domains of knowledge, reaches its maturity, and acquires its symmetry, as gradually and as surely as the oak is developed from the acorn. All accomplishments of a mushroom growth are the inventions of a modern and progressive epoch, and retard, rather than add to, the evolution of the mind's hidden powers.

After these general remarks upon the educational principles in vogue among the Moravians, and which are applicable to their male and female schools in Europe and in this country, I will conduct my readers to one of these institutions, which has become venerable by time, and by the respect it has inspired among all who have known and sustained it.

Plain and unenticing in its exterior, an abode of rural peace, surrounded by no worldly attractions, its popularity has been proportioned to its usefulness, and though of modest pretensions, and limited in its scale of operations, it will be found that therein lie the elements of its worth and endurance.

Let us now approach Nazareth Hall.[1]

---

[1] Of the various treatises upon education that have appeared among the Moravians of the last century, there was one by Bishop Layritz, which was held in high esteem when the intellectual was made more subservient to emotional knowledge than in these days; and as his precepts upon the instillment of practical lessons, and virtuous and religious principles, are curiously and quaintly given, I will furnish a specimen of one which relates to the education of the girl after she has left school and entered upon the duties of home life.

"The avocations to which a daughter should devote all her energies during these years include the whole household economy and all that pertains to household duties. The chief of these are spinning, knitting, cooking, washing, and working in the garden, etc.

"In all these female employments it is more urgent that she should be led into the useful than the ornamental. Thus it will be more needful for her to learn to cut out shirts and other linen clothing, and faithfully sew them, than to addict herself to patch-work, embroidery, and other fine needle-work. I do not say that the latter should be entirely neglected, if there be an opportunity for its exercise, but my aim is to have her first become skilled in what is really useful and indispensable. The same rule may be applied to all other female employments. Let your daughters avoid what is rare, handsome, and costly, which with them is generally the first object of attraction, and direct them chiefly to the serviceable, and exercise them so long on it as to enable them to produce a good piece of work. In spinning linen, cotton, and wool, instruct them how to divide the cuts, hanks, and skeins, according to usage, and also as to how much is required for a yard of linen; so that when they take it to the weaver they may know how much they have to claim of him.

"Here they can apply their knowledge of writing and ciphering. After they have been a certain time with their mother in the kitchen, and learned how to cook, then set them to cooking alone, and let their mother furnish them a weekly bill, so that they may learn by experience how much and what is needed for every meal, and when their resources fail, let them seek advice of their parent.

"In cooking, the same remark applies as to sewing, viz.: that the daughters should not be engaged in the skillful, or the choice and expensive, but adhere to the substantial, simple, and digestible dishes, and only indulge in the former for the sake of practice.

"As a matter of course, they should understand everything belonging to the kitchen, including the killing and dressing of poultry and fish. To this acquirement add the knowledge of the price of provisions, and how to proceed when they purchase them. The daughter can also keep a day-book, and charge her outlays, and her experience will teach her where her profit arises.

"In these years a faithful mother will instruct her in washing, and show her how to perform the whole operation of it, from soaking the clothes to the final drying and mangling. The worthy mother will see that her daughter does not overexert herself, but that she inures herself to labor by gradual efforts, and thus preserves her health and fits herself for future industry. The example of the parents will conduce greatly to show how she should conduct herself toward servants, and that she should neither give way to too much familiarity, nor exercise an air of too much authority among them.

"It will add much to her habits of order and punctuality, if the daughter is directed to make out a regular list of the pieces, so that when they are returned from the laundry, she can count them over, and lay them away on their respective shelves.

"And every year let the mother and the daughter go over the house-inventory, striking out of it whatever has disappeared, and adding whatever has been purchased. When, finally, all these things are accomplished under the eyes of the Lord, the education of the daughter under the mother's care will receive an enduring blessing from Him."

X.

NAZARETH HALL.

The old Boarding-school, known for the greater portion of a century as Nazareth Hall, stands in a commanding position, at the western side of the village, and in its southern view enjoys a landscape unsurpassed for beauty and fertility.

It was erected in 1755, for the purpose of accommodating Count Zinzendorf and his suite of fellow-pilgrims who accompanied him in his missionary labors, and as these resided with him in the capacity of coadjutors, this, in common with the designation of all other similar institutions, was intended as a "Disciple" or "Pilgrim House."

As the Count, after his visit in 1741, never returned to America, the large and imposing mansion was not used for its original design, and shortly before his death, in 1760, it was applied to the purposes to which it has ever since been dedicated. This early Boarding-school began in 1759 and lasted until 1779, during a part of which period it was large and flourishing; but from causes the enumeration of which would here be irrelevant, the operations of the Institution ceased for six years, when it was resuscitated under new auspices, (1785,) and has since remained, with the exception of some adverse stages, a successful undertaking.

The old Hall is a massive structure, built of blue limestone, (now covered over by a rough coating of gravel,) which formed the material of all the buildings of those early times. Its double-pitched roof, with two rows of dormer-windows, strengthens its claims to antiquity; and the balcony which crowns it is eagerly sought by the visitor, in order to study the surrounding prospect. During the hour preceding sunset, in a tranquil evening, the scene which nature here presents to her devoted student is beautiful in the extreme; and whether we look out upon the landscape from this balcony, or through the windows on the south side of the building, the senses become captivated by a harmonious picture.

In the course of modern progress many new suggestions have been thrown out to ornament the structure, in order to accommodate it to the wants and ideas of the times we live in; but in this brushing up of old walls, tearing off old panel-work, removing old balustrades, and effacing the marks on the stairs, which had been worn upon them by the feet of by-gone generations of boys, the antiquarian interest of the Hall has been, in some measure, diminished, and the change has called forth the regrets of all those whose affections and tastes derive their sustenance from the past. It belongs to the classic and refined perception to seek out that which is primitive, historical, and full of traditional story. To minds of this class elegant architecture affords but little attraction, and if it does, it only excites the intellect, without engaging the emotions. Let but some fragment of wood discover itself, which has been sanctified by age or the incidents of the past, and then the inanimate object becomes a thing of communication and thought.

Before the Hall underwent its late renovation, it had been the repeated victim of change, the various partition-walls in its second stories having often been torn down, in order to make large rooms small and small rooms large. Some years ago it was forced to submit to the fate of all venerable piles in this country, which must either be torn down or clothed in an entire new dress. Fortunately, its demolition was spared, but, much to the mortification of the antiquarian, it was metamorphosed into a comparatively modern looking structure. Notwithstanding this modernizing operation, it, however, still retains many of its lifeless memorials. In the small chapel, on the first floor, stand the four original octagonal columns that formed conspicuous objects in the old church, and which are associated with the recitations of the pupils on Examination-days, and between which all the old classic music of Haydn and Mozart was performed by the youthful amateur musicians. In the upper portion of the building, the roof, dormer-windows, balcony, and belfry, can all be identified, although much of the rest is lost to the eye, as it vainly seeks for that which it knew so well in boyhood.

Where the Corpse-house stood, there is now a vacant spot; but that solemn and mysterious structure which received the remains of those who were borne thither previous to interment, still vividly lives in the imagination, as it stood in rather close proximity to the Hall.

The venerable fountain which poured forth from the blue limestone reservoir, has been removed and placed under a more fanciful structure of painted lattice-work, contiguous to the Hall, quite near to one of the few remaining land-marks of the olden time, the large poplar tree, near the west end doorway. I deem this another instance of our defective taste, as the stone fountain in all the ancient European towns is one of their most characteristic features, and while the eternal waters of the earth continue to flow from it, the huge stone basins of granite or old gray marble indicate an age beyond the memory of man.

The square in front of the Hall, though deprived of many of its old poplars, still presents the same green area, now intersected and incompassed by walks, and nearly inclosed by buildings which have sprung up in recent times.

For the play-grounds of the boys, venerable and shady woods are reserved on the summit of the hill, in the rear of the town; but these woods have been sadly curtailed of their once natural and forest-like character, and no longer furnish the extensive range for the lads, who were wont to roam over them during the afternoon and twilight hours. The "Round Places" are still there, shaded over by the hickory, oak, and chestnut, and even by the very trees that stood there in days of yore; but as the eye scans the limits of the present grounds, it escapes through the interstices of the foliage into open fields all around, and the fact discloses itself that many old spots are entirely gone.

The garden, or pleasure-ground, possesses, probably, stronger claims to identity than any other spot or object remaining, as the old trees there constitute its great beauty and attraction. Its paths and its unique structures remain unaltered, and in strolling through this much-admired and cherished resort, the imagination of the pupil, who once held converse with them, falls irresistibly among the dreams and visions of the past. The garden was not at all times open to the boys, but they were admitted at special hours, their allotted recreation, as we have seen, having been at the "Round Places;" yet it was always free for visitors and citizens, and its shades were often chosen for idle hours.

Among things inanimate, an old and familiar friend was the bell, that hung for an age within the belfry, which still surmounts the Hall. This old favorite, in the days of our youth, was well known for its habit of telling the quarters before it told the hours, and, lingering in the garden, or in the woods above the graveyard, those gentle sounds of one, two, and three quarters fell upon the ear with the force of significant and expressive music. In these monotonous tones of the modest quarter bell, the denizen of the Hall as well as of the hamlet enjoyed much comfort, and whenever he missed the sounds for a time, he was glad to hear them again. In its new abode, the same old clock is heard to proclaim the quarters, but from its changed position, its effect on the visitor is in part lost, as it no longer retains the perfect identity looked for in the recognition of old and cherished objects.

During recitation hours, Time, under this impersonation, was an important actor, as the telling of the hours, and especially of the last four quarters, drove away suspense on the part of the diffident school-boy, who may not have been well prepared, or on whom the irksomeness of hard study was an onerous burden. By all such, the final fourth quarter was listened to with restless suspense, and when the eventful "four o'clock" pealed forth, a general shout announced the close of the school day.

A staunch regulation in old Moravian life was the custom of dining precisely at 12 M. With this view the bell was punctually rung at "three-quarters," as it was called, or a quarter of an hour preceding the event. This made the hour of the meal perfectly uniform throughout the Hall and village, and as the three-quarter bell rung, the laborer was seen bending his steps homeward, on the important errand of cheering the inner man.

There was another "three-quarters" just before eight in the morning, which gave intelligence to all within and without the Hall, that the hour for school was near at hand, and forced many a fearful youth to brace his nerves for the coming occasion, when, with a partially learned lesson, he was to enter the presence of a dreaded tutor. To that noted bell, therefore, we owe many grateful and heart-awakening memories, for it was the arbiter of important events in the visits of Time to the soul of youth, and the aged still feel a pleasure in listening to the tones it sends forth, although summoning the lads of another generation to its momentous calls.

I have already, under a different head, alluded to the nature of the recreations indulged in by the pupils, and shall endeavor to present them here more in detail, although they are characteristic of most of our schools, and are only modified by the requirements of sex; yet in the sketch of Nazareth Hall, all its peculiar pastimes form a portion of its chronicles. And these chronicles are not to be overlooked, for the pastimes, the games in the woods, and the walks in the environs, are the green spots within the memories of all the old men who were once pupils there. In the summer season, the swimming excursions on Wednesday and Saturday afternoons, those immemorial semi-weekly holidays, were matters of great desire and enjoyment. The tutor, with his "Room" of clamorous youth, who, long ere the hour of two arrived, became impatient to go forth to the Bushkill,[1] might be seen departing on a "swimming," regularly on each of those afternoons. With "swimming-breeches," as they were styled in the nomenclature of the Hall, towel and soap, and dressed in the nonchalant attire of boys upon a hot day, the merry groups repaired to some well-known "Deep Hole," sufficient for the purpose of making the primary attempts at bathing. On the return from the scene of ablution, a well-known stopping place used to present itself at Nisky, where the good dame came forth with pots of cold milk, pies, and buttered-bread, to regale the appetites sharpened to their utmost acuteness by health-giving air, exercise, and aquatic sports.

At a later day, and, indeed, at the time I am writing, the pond at Boulton is the exclusive resort for all these purposes, and the first inquiry made by the boys, on their arrival there, is for the "boat-key," to enable them to unchain that most important instrument of the day's amusement, and sail on the

---

[1] Bushkill, or Lehictan, a beautiful and romantic stream, on which, three miles distant from Nazareth, are situated Boulton gun works.

waters. Accompanying these excursions may generally be seen a baggage-wagon, well provisioned, and fully appointed with all the culinary equipment requisite for a whole day's encampment in the woods. The appearance of the team, as it moves along the road, drawing the car with a long rope, similar to that of a fire-engine, is a merry spectacle, and the arrival at Boulton, within sight of the water, is generally announced by a hearty cheer, indicative of the good state of feeling among the boys, who are like birds just released from the cage.

Far up among the winding recesses of the stream there are found romantic retreats, where the hemlock and laurel overhang and shade it. Here the boys select some quiet nook for their collations, which receive additional zest from the fish and frogs caught during the day. Among the dense thickets of laurel a fire is lighted to prepare the meal, boil the coffee, etc., imparting to the tableau the appearance of a gipsy encampment. Such entertainments as are here enjoyed give relish to the tedium of academic life; these healthful out-door recreations invigorate the system and impart buoyancy to the temperament, and, to prevent its sinking, they should always be indulged in to an extent compatible with a judicious and lenient discipline.

During the autumn, when the leaf of the forest turns to its sere and yellow hues, new interest is felt for the arrival of four P.M., and each boy, armed with bag and club, strikes into the woods to gather the wild offerings of the season. This portion of out-door life has its never-failing joys, and I have known boys to lay up during those days of brown autumn stores of nuts for esculent purposes, which have excited the envy of many a gray squirrel. To discuss these nuts becomes the employment of the winter months, and they prove an excellent solace for the deprivation of the higher luxuries of home. They cost much personal labor, and involve many adventures in gathering them.

Having laid up these winter stores, due preparations are now made for the scene that soon discloses itself in the snow-clad fields and icy ponds in the vicinity. Descending on sleds is a daily amusement, and Wednesday and Saturday afternoons enable the "Rooms" to go out and enjoy sledding and skating in all their glory. These parties are, probably, the merriest in the yearly round of amusements, and the recollection of them in the minds of those who revert to them, is always glowing and cheerful. The most intensely cold days are braved with indifference, and the young life-blood warms to the highest point the enthusiasm of those inspiring pleasures. But, perhaps, the general sleigh-ride by all the "Rooms," is the most exciting occurrence of the year, (always excepting Examination-day and departure for home.)

In more primitive days, on the first appearance of a deep fall of snow, it was customary, on the

18*

afternoon preceding the grand fête, to go out among the neighboring farmers and engage a full cavalcade of sleighs, sufficient for the accommodation of the whole school. A party of one hundred required a considerable muster, and, before the modern encroachments of luxury and taste, with paint, arabesque and gilding, and buffaloe and tiger skins, had crept into the country, the old-fashioned stiff-backed sleigh, with the home-made party-colored coverlet trailing behind, was often introduced into the merry train. The steeds, often past the meridian of life, and educated to toil rather than pleasure, and the drivers, innocent of the dangers that Bellerophon had encountered, yet all seemed inspired by the occasion, and the grand signal for departure was given, followed by the music of the bells, the cheers of the boys, and the acclamations of the spectators. For the stopping-place, some inn was generally selected where the cuisine stood in fair repute, and to which due notice of the number of the party and the hour of arrival had been sent the day before.

All these events are written as the things of a past day, yet the customs of which they formed a part still survive, under modified forms, but imbued with as jovial indications of youth as ever. The old-fashioned sleigh, with its coverlet, has given place to the ample omnibus and four, driven by an adept, with a full supply of dark fur robes, and miniature bells in numberless strings in lieu of the large one formerly dangling beneath the horse's neck; all mark a new age in the outward circumstances of life, although the heart and its joys, youth and its predilections, remain as ever, bright and cloudless.

Among other things now passed away, was the celebration of teachers' and principals' Birth-day. The former was generally made the occasion of an afternoon party in one of the "Rooms," and participated in by a few teachers, over coffee, cigars, and buns; while the boys belonging to the same Room, and seated at their long tables, enjoyed that part of the luxury which related to the coffee and buns. This "Vesper," as the collation was termed, was a convivial one, and was an offspring of Moravian life which, as already seen, makes the Birthday a prominent and happy event.

There is no record left to show when the last of these joyous afternoons was observed, but, together with the "Inspector's turkey-feast," on the occasion of his own anniversary, they are now deemed obsolete.

In 1855 the Examination and the Centenary Anniversary of the erection of the Hall were celebrated on the same day.

To give a becoming acknowledgment to this event, the boys decorated all their "Rooms" with oak-leaf garlands and inscriptions on the walls, indicative of the day, the vacation and its pleasures. In the chapel, prepared by the hands of the tutors, were beautiful devices of hemlock wreaths, roses, and flowers, illustrative of the jubilee to which the

Hall had attained, and, at the same time, animating the "Examination" by a twofold solemnity. The Hall had just reached its hundredth year of existence; it had been occupied as a boarding-school nearly all that time, and had sent forth from its tutelage fourteen hundred pupils. In the recitation and musical department, unusual exertions had been made by the preceptors to fill up the pleasure of the day, and every one seemed gratified.

The outer symbols of the affections and rejoicings, which we recognize in the hemlock, the laurel, the wild moss, and the oak-leaf, fashioned into simple designs and classic wreaths, have ever been a happy result of art, as inculcated in the Hall, and it is to be hoped that these characteristic features may be preserved, and go down unchanged to the youth of many generations yet to come.

I have already hinted that the garden retained its identity more than any other spot; but even here, many time-worn resting-places have been shorn of their attractions, and transformed into new rural conceptions. These well-known seats should be suffered to remain, be they ever so primitive or rudely constructed, until the tooth of time shall have gnawed away everything that is left of them. They are the truest depositories of our youthful susceptibilities, and when we come to seek them out, after long absence, the present is completely merged in the past.

An old and cherished resort of the pupils of the

earlier part of the present century was "*Sacred to Meditation*," the designation of a summer-house near the oval pond, which it overlooked, and which has since been superseded by a grass plot. This was always occupied by some congenial conclave, discoursing on themes that most interested the youthful imagination, in the full play of boyish fancy and frivolity. At the extremity of the avenue, which first admits the visitor into the garden through a huge revolving gate, surmounted by the well-known eagle, with its outspread wings, there formerly stood another summer-house, containing a panel painting. It was the clever production of some forgotten landscape artist, perhaps belonging to the Hall, and described a pastoral scene, the details of which have now worn off from my memory. It long withstood the ravages of the atmosphere and the vandalism of the boys, until, eventually, it became so defaced that its figures could no longer be recognized. This was a chosen locality for many of the pupils of the olden time, and the very defacements of the picture strengthened their attachment to it. Over the massive stone walls that inclose the spring a balcony is now erected for the use of the musicians, who often perform on festival days.

Of the trees that formerly lent their grateful shadows to the denizens of this hallowed spot, the greater part yet remain, noble and beautiful in their old age. The gaunt and ungraceful form of the American elm is still to be seen near the "Reservoir," while above it we find the stately and towering white pines and beech. In strolling among the trees, the visitor recognizes, on all sides, a host of old acquaintances in these arborescent figures; and, although age has swelled their proportions into increased size and stature, they address the mind by the same medium of intelligence they were always wont to do. On the beech, a well-known and ready victim of the pocket-knife everywhere, many initials may yet be traced of boys who flourished here a quarter of a century ago; but where such incisions were made at an earlier date, they have been consigned to oblivion by the tree, whose monumental trust scarcely exceeds a score of years.

In revisiting the village, the former pupil will miss many a well-known face, but in an hour's stroll through the garden, he will find the English elm, the ash, the beech, the pine, the copse of juniper, the larch, the catalpa, the poplars, the willows near the stream, the same underwood, the same flowers, grasses, and mosses so familiar to him when he dwelt among them.

In connection with the Hall, we must not pass the Sisters' House unnoticed, for, from the part it acted in the cuisine, it occupies an important place in the memories of the older pupils. Here, for a long time, flourished the "kitchen department," from which the meals were carried to the Hall refectory by the Sisters, who were aided by the boys in the capacity of "Week-holders," an office which, every Saturday night, was assumed, for one week, by two boys of each "Room." Many pleasing pictures of the Moravian maiden Sister, sitting in industrious silence, innocent of the world's attractions, happy and elevated to the inner element of Christian life and contemplation, were found here, and are still referred to by those who seek out former acquaintances. With these the boys cultivated an intercourse for the sake of a favorite mint-cake, and repaired regularly to the Sisters' House for those invaluable confections. The Sisters' House and its out-buildings, sombre and somewhat dilapidated, still remain, and preserve their quaint picture unaltered and uneffaced.

Examination-days are yet what they ever were. The same exercises engage the efforts of the pupils, and similar scenes are enacted over again at the departure for home. In the "Square," the busy scene is still beheld, of leave-taking, heaping up trunks, last adieus, hurras for home, and all the other accompaniments of the close of the session. Sad hearts, as ever, linger behind within the silent walls, looking on the gay spectacle before them, and repining at their own lot, which dooms them to remain, while others depart with visions of enjoyment in store.

Since the day of which I was a part, some changes have taken place in the exterior of life, in the conventionalities of thought, and in the general observances of society; yet here youthful ebullitions come up from the same spring they ever did, and the heart's fountains, like the deep sources of the mountain brook, remain the same throughout all time.

As soon as the "Examination" is over, and the "Vacation" has arrived, liberty lends wings to the youthful captive, and he feels like an unchained being. During a four weeks' respite, he can throw aside the shackles that bound him, and his allegiance to preceptor and to school.

Many return with pleasure to their adopted home, the abode of learning, where the foundation of early affection of both mind and heart is first laid, and the attachment to the Hall endures for a triennial stay there. But as the boy develops and strides forward toward manhood, his yearnings for the larger pursuits and ambitions of life come on, his wishes increase upon him, and he gradually tires under the confinement of his Alma Mater.

This is probably as it must be, but even in three or four years the discipline of this peculiar school will tell upon future character. Of all its *elèves* who have gone forth to occupy the position in society which Providence may have assigned them, few, it is gratifying to observe, have dishonored the institution that fostered their juvenile years. Few, it is true, ever reached that high eminence which, in the acceptation of the world's vocabulary, is called fame; yet if we follow their career along those ordinary paths where true merit and genuine worth find their own rewards, we shall see that, without reaching any dazzling eminence or pride of place, on them the Hall, the good tree of wisdom and decorous demeanor, always left fall its grateful fruits. In looking over the career and fate of others, we may find that life proved a shipwreck of the virtues and the early inculcations of religion, even to the tender nursling of Moravian paternity; but if the eye could have reached the deep recesses of the heart of those fallen ones, doubtless, secret yearnings for that Arcadia of their youth could have been discerned.

XI.

ENVIRONS OF NAZARETH.

In leaving the Hall, its inmates, their duties and their pleasures, it will be worth our attention to look around and see what is left of the original Nazareth itself, as it stood when the scenes of which I have given a sketch took place.

Something of the original village may be conceived, by visiting, here and there, an antiquated house, that has withstood the inroads of time and the encroachments of modern architecture. Few of these, however, remain; the village itself having, by constant renovation, become completely modernized. The antiquarian in these matters of early Moravian vestiges feels an interest in researches connected with them, for the tale of Moravian life was marked, poetical and picturesque.

The old cemetery beyond the boys' play-ground may still be traced, although it was suffered to fall into neglect, the land it occupied having been sold, and, for want of sufficient interest in it, no proper measures were taken to secure in perpetuity this old and remarkable burial-place. A few of the broken and fragmentary slabs, with defaced names upon them, have been rescued and preserved in the room of the Moravian Historical Society. It was here that interments from Ephrata, the "Rose," and Old Nazareth took place, and during the appalling times of Indian warfare, the funeral procession often moved in fear, and required an armed guard for an escort into the woods. Standing alone, in its solitary reality, that ancient burial-ground might have proved an object of thoughtful meditation, for it gave a resting-place to some of those early pioneers and Indian converts whose names it would be pleasant to read, and which the pilgrim to that silent spot would gladly seek.

A little south of the cemetery are the most favorite and noted views the environs of Nazareth furnish. From Gnadenthal Hill, lying but a short walk's distance west of the play-ground, the southern panorama presents itself, and will repay the visitor for his ramble thither. Far as the vision reaches, can be seen an intermingling of hills and champaign country, dotted with small settlements and farm-houses, and inclosed along the southern and western horizon by the Lehigh Hills and the Blue Ridge.

The Gnadenthal Hills have always been a cherished resort, both to the strolling student, in search of a fine pictorial study, and to the gay school-boy troop, who were wont to cross them in autumn to visit the orchards of "Old Schlabach," and take home liberal supplies of apples. And when the chestnuts ripened, this was the scene of action for the busy lads who sought the coveted fruit of the beautiful tree that crowns the summits of these hills.

In addition to the view from this western point, the picture around the play-grounds is engrossing to the wanderer over this well-trodden ground. Its beauty was never lost upon the contemplation of the tutor, as he sat on a rustic bench during the plays of the boys, and the latter themselves, after the absence of half a lifetime, seek the spot to realize once more that which, implanted in the early imagination, becomes a subsequent day-dream.

If the sojourner here wish to extend his researches, and feast upon the pictures around, let him drive out through the ancient and still lingering remnant of the Moravian village of Christianspring. In this excursion he will pass the site of Gnadenthal, now converted into the County Alms-House, but still preserving one or more of the original structures that composed the place. In the visit to Christianspring, he will discover the ancient houses as they always stood, but for a key to their design and history, he must refer to oral information and written chronicles. The same may be said of the whole ramble around Nazareth and its environs. The curious explorer should be versed in the history, the incidents and the characters of an early period, and be imbued with some feelings of admiration for their moral achievements.

Two pleasant retreats, known as the "John Spring," and the "Lundt Spring," are engraven upon that same tablet on which so much has already been written, for they were favorite resorts during moments of liberty from the enthrallments of study, and even in this late day of the life of many a former pupil, these springs and their gurgling waters call up visions of the morning of their manhood.

The "John Spring," which was inclosed within a small hollow, or ravine, at the termination of the "Round Place," surrounded and sheltered overhead by dense foliage of oaks and chestnuts, not only attracted the school-boy to its sequestered and lonely shades, but in the stroll around Nazareth it always became a point of attraction. But in visiting at this time what was formerly known as "John Spring," it is difficult to recognize where that favorite spot was, and where that cool spring oozed out of the hill beneath the spreading shade of those old trees; for those well-known trees have all been leveled with the ground, the ploughshare has been there, and open fields and glaring sunbeams have driven away the twilight stillness that was so long its charm.

In exploring the localities known as the "Lundt Spring," we shall find that nature has for once retained her mastery, and that little has been done by the hand of man to mar her primitive beauty. The "Lundt Spring," lying deep down in a ravine, to the north of the village, preserves its romantic identity.

The old "Bore Spring" still issues forth perpendicularly out of the same perforation once made for it, and whence tradition says it spouted up some feet in height; and, as we tread the paths in the vicinity of the noted fountain, the dark slate rocks fringed with moss and ferns, and rare wild flowers, still lend a picturesque aspect to the sides of the hill.

The "Lundt Spring" is a place well adapted for parties of pleasure, and is often made available for that purpose. It is also resorted to by the lover of solitude and study, and as it is, to all appearances, unassailable by the hand of utility and improvement, it will probably long flourish in its primeval wildness. Although the woodman's dreaded axe is fast approaching, and is occasionally heard near and around it, sweeping from the earth the genius of poesy and imagination, and following alone the rude instincts of necessity and material wants, yet this solitary fountain, amid the concealments of venerable oaks and its rocky defile, will, let us hope, be long held sacred by the coming generation. The villagers have reserved the grounds that inclose the spring, and with rude seats, and paths, and rural architecture, have rendered the spot inviting to the pleasure-seeker who loves to stray into the quiet woods, where can be heard no sounds but those of birds or or of the dripping waters of some cool spring.

A short walk south of the "Whitefield House," or Ephrata, leads to the site of Old Nazareth. The ancient building that constituted the chief abode of the early inhabitants has recently been removed, after having stood for a long time, attracting the gaze of the curious, and inviting many an explorer of our antiquities to its interior, to discover that rude, quaint, and primitive workmanship, in which the hands of one of the first and most remarkable Moravians, of him who felled the first tree for the building of Herrnhut, were engaged. That man was Christian David.

Passing through the gateway, formerly guarded by the "Two Lindens,"[1] but now by their successors,

---

[1] For a long time those two lindens stood, majestic consorts, overhanging the gateway, and were objects of great attraction. The "corpse-house" was in close proximity to them, and the funereal scene, just before the procession moved onward to the cemetery, was enacted under their boughs. Here the boys played, and their recollections of the Hall and its surroundings are enlivened by the noble trees that shaded their sports, and became the objects of their boyish attachments. Old Father Schäfer, who lived near the Square, in the little stone-house, which, to this day, stands in its pristine simplicity and humility, became, in a measure, immortalized by having unconsciously performed the meritorious deed of planting those two trees. No chronicle of the occurrence being within my reach, it is not in my power to say how long ago this took place; but the greater part of a century must have elapsed since the date of the event.

Father Schäfer, as he was wont to pass the Hall, to and fro, became known to the boys as the worthy who planted the lindens; and in 1855, when the Reunion of the old pupils took place, there was a reverential mention made of him, in recalling the images of the two trees that now could no longer be seen; for decay having come upon them, and ren-

and through an avenue of English elms, of recent growth, and climbing the ascent leading past the garden, we are brought to the cemetery. Immediately over the entrance are the words from

---

dered them unsafe occupants of the place which they had adorned, they shortly before had been felled to the ground. Here they stood, the janitors of the gateway, and as we passed into the pleasure-grounds, or if we stood upon the summit of the hill and looked down upon the village and its environs, the two huge lindens were objects of glad recognition.

Those old acquaintances are gone. For some years their stumps were still examined by the curious pilgrim, but, during the summer of 1857, the old pupils, assembling on the venerated spot, decided on replacing the lindens by planting, with all due ceremony, two nurslings, which, we hope, many of the living youth, who assisted in the transaction, may live to see grow up into a sturdy old age.

The two original lindens have had many to lament their fall, as the boys of thirty and forty years ago, feeling the glow of rejuvenescence within them, have returned to revel in the past, and become young again, by culling the flowers of departed days. Many of those flowers, it is true, have lost their fragrance; they smell sweetly no more, as they did when a merry boyhood knew no bitterness; still they are beautiful to the soul, and the heart of the grown-up man feels chastened as he gathers them.

What the eventual fate of the lindens was, I never learned; whether their trunks were sacrilegiously used for fuel, or piously preserved, history does not say; yet the important position they occupied in the memory, and the strong hold they had upon the veneration of all who knew them, made them deserving of a better fate than probably befell them.

Scripture: "Because I lived, ye shall live also;"[1] intimating that those who are borne through that passage shall, for a short time, be seen no more, but that the death, which is thought to seal up all earthly hopes and aspirations, is only a transient sleep, and a preparation for a bright reunion of kindred spirits. Its chosen situation on the summit of the hill, where the eye looks down on Nazareth and takes in the whole landscape, has always made it distinguished among our burial-places. The ground is laid out in a manner similar to that of all the Moravian cemeteries, one-half allotted to each sex. Each grave is covered with a large, oblong marble slab, bearing the name, age, place of nativity, and of death. Around the mound that marks the grave, humble flowers are planted and nurtured, and of these the wild thyme is a well-known favorite. Within late years trees have been added, and will in time become the chief interest and attraction of the grounds.

This sacred spot, with its ancient graves, whose inscriptions tell of many names that were connected with the annals of Nazareth, is not unworthy of contemplation; and if the mind of the visitor has fallen into a proper mood by the chaste and solemn impressions of the ground he treads upon, the study of the whole outward world will receive increased effect. Of

---

[1] This inscription above the gateway is in imitation of the Herrnhut Cemetery, where a similar quotation is placed overhead, in entering its silent portals.

late years one of the aged denizens of the village has taken the burial-place into his peculiar charge, selecting and planting the trees, improving the walks, and gently letting down into their small narrow cells many of those whose lot it is to be carried thither. Having himself already reached the patriarchal age, and seeing that the horizon of this earthly sphere is gradually drawing closer, he seems to take a pleasure in adorning that quiet place on the summit of the hill, where he too shall, ere long, be borne.

Of the various strolls around Nazareth, not the least inviting is that in the direction of Friedensthal, an ancient settlement of the Moravians, where their old mill yet occupies its former site, although the original buildings around it have disappeared. The road in this direction leads through the settlement known by the name of Nisky, a rural cluster of cottages of singular comfort and neatness, so that the passer-by is almost tempted to step in and see how life is spent in such abodes. Here the earth teems with fruits, and the community seems to sit in the lap of fertility. No display of art is seen to grace the dwellings, but the character of the spot breathes that species of tranquil comfort which belongs to an unassuming rural abode. No place can be found in this vicinity to vie with Nisky, in all the requisites of a charming picture, and as we pass its cottages, with smiling verdure, fruitful drapery and shady trees, grouped around, we feel disposed to cultivate an acquaintance with them.

Among these old cottages, there is, at the extremity of the village, one that is rendered remarkable as the former hospice of the boys, when they returned from bathing, of which I have made mention while recounting their aquatic feats. The domicile stands in its primitive aspect, surrounded by its green lawn, and shaded by its fruit-trees, as in days of yore. But the inmates who then ministered to the school-boys' wants, and opened the door of hospitality, are no more—both, in their appointed time, have gone the way of all the earth, and their remains been deposited in the beautiful cemetery.

XII.

EPHRATA.

In the eastern portion of the village of Nazareth stands an old gray edifice, the appearance of which betokens some peculiar origin, and naturally awakens an inquiry in the mind of the stranger as to its history and purposes.

This is the "Whitefield House." For more than one hundred years it stood quite alone, having but two humble log-huts in close proximity to it, and, in company with those, it overlooked that same wide, unrivaled domain I have already pointed out from the terrace of the Hall. This venerable mansion is a solid structure, built of limestone in the most durable style of masonry, and fitted to resist, for a long time, the assaults of corroding age. It faces a lawn of quiet aspect, and the view from its upper windows is only equaled by that from the Hall or the precincts of the cemetery. This group of houses, with its allotted portion of land, is called "Ephrata;" and as it may be considered the cradle of Moravianism in America, I shall, after having led my reader through Herrnhut, and sketched the life and character of its founder, Zinzendorf, introduce it to his attention.

After Spangenberg, with his small party of ten persons, had led the way to our shores, we have seen that he was soon followed by another company, of twenty emigrants, who settled in the vicinity of Savannah in the year 1735. Without effecting any permanent colony, they were, at last, in consequence of hostilities between the province and the Spaniards, obliged to forsake the place. But before leaving Georgia a few of them became intimately acquainted with George Whitefield, who persuaded those who were good mechanics to go to the northern wilds of Pennsylvania and there, on a tract of land, five thousand acres in extent, erect a large building which he designed as a school for colored orphan children. The Brethren who undertook this task were named Antes, Seifert, and Boehler. When they arrived at the designated place, they found themselves in the vicinity of an Indian village, where afterwards was "Old Nazareth," long marked by its original appearance, and the quaintness of its curiously-built German-looking houses.

On their first visit to this little opening in the wilderness, the pioneers slept under an oak-tree, the roots of which are still traced out by one of our devoted antiquaries, and of which a few fragments are piously preserved. He points out the spot where, down in the meadow, a little distance north of Ephrata, stood the memorable tree; and, should any one feel an interest in exploring to their source these historical matters, I will refer him to the "Antiquary of Nazareth." It was under this tree they terminated their day's toil by songs of praise, which, unfortunately, have not been preserved, else it would be gratifying to record them here.

In an interview with Whitefield, who was then at Philadelphia, having left Georgia at the same time with the Moravian company, they settled the terms of their contract with him, and then, with their families, they returned to Ephrata, to proceed with the construction of the building. As winter came on before the completion of the house, the foundations of which could only be laid up to the first story, log buildings were hastily thrown up, and the settlers remained within them until the ensuing spring, when differences arising between them and Whitefield, the place was forsaken, and the whole company, including an additional arrival from Germany, proceeded to a tract of five hundred acres that had been purchased on the Lehigh, and now the site of Bethlehem. This event occurred in 1741, the year following the commencement of Ephrata, the building of which was not resumed and completed until 1743, when the Brethren purchased of Whitefield the whole five thousand acres of land. This will suffice as the preliminary history of Ephrata, and I have unavoidably introduced it here, as it opens to view the first permanent settlement of the Moravians in this country.

During the last hundred and fifteen years, the antique pile has passed through many vicissitudes, and has been appropriated to various uses. The most important of these was, for a long time, that of a "Nursery" for the infant children between two and three years, and even younger, who were placed in the public charge, after having been taken from their parents, who were, by the exigencies of those trying times, forced to this measure, in order to be enabled the better to labor for the common good of the community.

The sensibilities of a modern and effeminate age, like our own, will hardly be reconciled to this remarkable phase in the character and history of those early Moravian Brethren, and no religious ends would seem to justify a species of martyrdom such as it was. But it is difficult to realize the position in which the German emigrants of that day really stood, or to conceive the actual hardships they had to undergo in order to obtain the necessaries of life. The nursery system, I am happy to say, was, after a course of years, abandoned, and Ephrata was applied to other purposes.

The interior of the building exhibits that rudeness of construction and material which were the result of those primitive times. The wood-work, although recently covered with a coating of paint, showed, for more than a century, nothing but the dingy color of the oaken boards, which had been sawed by hand out of the forest tree. The little porch, before the entrance to the south side, is of the same rude unpainted material, as is also the frame-work of the windows. The sills of the upper and lower doors are made of a finely variegated soapstone, reputed to have been brought from abroad, and at one time rumored to be of alabaster, but with what correctness I cannot say.

The site of Ephrata and Nazareth seems to have been judiciously chosen, for the remarkable fertility of all the adjacent lands has rendered this a country equal in productiveness to any portion of Pennsylvania; while a glance from the upper apartments of the Ephrata House across the surrounding farms and woodland scenery will fascinate the eye with their beauty.

Though the hand of change and innovation is now doing its work all around, Ephrata itself is still held sacred, and the rude and callous reformer forbears to touch it. While formerly it was a quiet retreat, off from the wayside, as you passed on to the village of Nazareth, now the place is almost absorbed by the town itself, and its air no longer is that of perfect and undisturbed seclusion.

At some distance north of the Whitefield House stood, until recently, a solitary building called "The Rose," which was a place of refuge while the Indians had possession of the surrounding country, and was used by the Brethren as an inn and store, previous to the erection of such places of public accommodation in Nazareth itself.

Below Ephrata, on the site of the old Indian village, which our three adventurers found there, Old Nazareth was commenced in 1744, and was the scene of some of the early operations of the primitive people. The traditions of those early days are occasionally drawn forth from some surviving descendant of the settlers, and among these I have found one relating to the "Rose."

It was customary to have all the cakes for that establishment supplied from the Old Nazareth bakery, and a little girl was charged with transporting them on a wheelbarrow out to the "Rose." On these occasions the Indians, who infested the neighborhood, frequently attacked this "transportation line," seized the wheelbarrow, trundled it to some distance, to terrify the little creature, and then restored it to her again.

It is also told, and I made some reference to it when speaking of the ancient burial-ground, that the early interments often took place under an escort of armed men, who proceeded with the corpse from the "Rose" to the "Hutberg," as it was then called.

The "Rose" itself now presents nothing more of its former appearance than its mere locality, which is prettily chosen, and commands a fine southern view, embracing Ephrata, Nazareth, and the Lehigh hills.

The walk between the two places, Ephrata and the "Rose," through a large portion of woods, in old times, must have been a delightful one, passing over in part what was then termed the "King's Highway," a main road running east of Ephrata and north from Nazareth.

In a few years after the erection of the Ephrata Mansion and Old Nazareth, the village of Nazareth proper was commenced, with the Hall, and, subsequently, the Sisters' House and other buildings. The husbandman cleared away the forest, became master of the fields, and the sway of the red man was no more. The last relics of the aboriginal were left to be turned up by the plow for many years afterwards; and, indeed, have not yet escaped the scrutiny of the school-boy, in the jasper-colored arrow-heads. Of these, large numbers have been picked up, and treasured as mementoes of savage life.

Upon the lawn in front, in the olden time, many pleasant scenes took place, connected with the solemnities of the church. One of the most interesting of these was the general "Love-Feast" of the congregation, on the day of the laying of the corner-stone of Nazareth Hall.

It is still left to explain more fully the origin of the two small block-houses, mentioned above as belonging to the Ephrata group. These aged-looking objects were thrown up in the winter of 1740, or, as our most reliable antiquary will have it, one of them only, and the other in 1743, for the shelter of the little company who wintered there. The oak timber, of which they are composed, is yet in a tolerably good state of preservation; and if those who have the control of the property should let their respect of the past remain in the ascendency, the humble structures, the first refuge of our pilgrim fathers in this portion of the New World, may stand a long while. Their sharp peaked roofs, small windows and frame-work, already distorted by the force of time, their dusky look, and the rude, unhewn log-work on one of them,—all serve to mark them as some peculiar results of a period that has now become historical.

In standing before these houses, the interest in them is not a little increased by the reflection, that during the winter of their first occupancy Bishop David Nitschmann, old Father Nitschmann, and Anna Nitschmann, whose history and character I have already referred to, arrived here, and resided with the other party till the ensuing spring. During this period, the latter had resigned her important office of Eldress at Herrnhaag, in order to travel to a distant country, brave the terrors of the sea, and traverse savage wilds, such as the interior of Pennsylvania might be regarded at the eventful period intervening between 1740 and 1760.

If we suffer our imagination to place us, during that winter, in a spot so far removed from the precincts of civilization, we shall receive additional light on the subject of the Moravian enterprise during its incipient stages. The Nitschmanns had expatriated themselves from their native country, Moravia, had gone to Herrnhut, and joined the renewed church of the Brethren, and thence proceeded to the great work of the mission, by going forth, personally, to explore distant lands. The missionary of those days was cast upon his own resources; the women were given to industrious pursuits, and generally the men were able mechanics; and while they dwelt within an inner sphere, their outward life was one of hardship and probation.

Small and obscure as the Moravian work seemed to be, at the time when Ephrata was the only beacon-light that presented itself to this handful of pilgrims, as they traced the paths into the unfrequented quarters inhabited only by the Indians, the gradual success that everywhere, at all accessible points of the earth, attended it, proved the wise guidance by which its great purposes were led.

In walking from the "Rose," or, rather, from the spot where it once was, the antiquated Ephrata House, with its sombre and significant exterior, and its many historical associations, looms up before us. Although this monument of a past time is nearly surrounded by the unattractive and commonplace facts of the day, and of the times in which we move and take a part, yet the spirit of that same past hovers over and protects it.

XIII.

BETHLEHEM.

It was early in the year 1741, that the small body of Moravians, seventeen in number, who, during the winter of 1740, occupied the log-house in Ephrata, proceeded to the River Lehigh to take possession of the five hundred acres of land they had purchased of Mr. Allen. At that time the Indian stream, known by the name of Lecha, ran peacefully through the mazes of a forest, along the ridges of mountains called by the same name.

When the first axe was raised to clear the site of this new colony, there were on or near the river but two habitations of the whites, together with a few scattered Indian wigwams. During a cold December evening of this memorable year, a small company might have been seen assembled in the obscure log-hut, which, with a stable attached to one end of it, had been first thrown up to meet the wants of the settlers. Among this assembly were Count Zinzendorf and his daughter Benigna, who had just arrived in America, had found their way to these wilds, and joined the body of pilgrims who had wintered at Ephrata, and the chief characters among whom I have named. The scene here presented was a Christmas-eve in the woods, and on that eventful night the Moravian hymn of Zinzendorf's own composition was heard to rise out of the hut, uttered by the voices of that choir of devoted Christians, their hearts filled with increased interest from the coincidence that the Christmas celebration was performed in part within a stable. The proposed name of the settlement had been Bethlechem, or house on the Lecha, but as the scenes of Bethlehem, in Judea, on the night of the Saviour's nativity, had just been commemorated, it was suggested it should be changed to Bethlehem.

In the following year, 1742, a large house was completed for the accommodation of the infant congregation, and new accessions coming in from Europe, the village gradually swelled in size.

The aboriginal, who was then the occupant of this wild domain, soon came within the softening influence of the gospel introduced by the Moravian Brethren, became a convert to Christianity, and a friend to the cause and interests of the small band of emigrants who took possession of this spot. Subsequently, those tribes, who were not in the immediate vicinity of the Moravian settlement, and who were opposed to the Christian converts, either through the animosity so apt to be entertained by a separate people, or from opposition to the English, being under French influence, proved offensive and dangerous to the inhabitants of Bethlehem, and frequent incursions were made toward and against the place. To ward off these dangers all the vigilance of its inhabitants were exercised, and their escape from massacre and total extinction is one of the miracles of their history. It is related of those early times, that the Sisters would at one time be in the field gathering flax, when the Indians, approaching by stealth, endeavored to make them their prey; at another time, ignited wads would be discharged into the thatched roofs of the houses, in order to set them on fire. In addition to this, the Indian converts were in jeopardy from the government itself, as the English had offered a high reward for an Indian scalp, which rendered it hazardous for any of the uncivilized people who enjoyed the protection of Bethlehem, to venture far into the forest, as their death would be the inevitable penalty, should they fall into the hands of a white or savage enemy.

The red man, who was thus domiciled and domesticated among the Moravians, soon became attached to the new mode of life he had assumed and the new religion he had adopted in exchange for that which he had laid aside. The services for the Indian audience were performed in their own language, translations being provided for them, and every facility was afforded for the proper comprehension of that

Divine instruction, which now, for the first time, threw a flood of light upon their souls. In reading these passages of Moravian life, where the Indian group engrosses the picture, we are struck with the unique and marked peculiarity of the people whose history and fame we are thus cursorily dwelling upon.

The period that characterized early Bethlehem was one of the poetical phases in the history of our race, and although the modes and associations of life were rude, the aims were purely spiritual, and every individual was endowed with inner impulses. As the imagination carries us back to that period, we hear a solemn chaunt, the music of the Moravian hymn, in the Mohican tongue. The actors in this scene are in primitive costume, modified by intercourse with the whites; and as the anthem ascends on high, or the Christian prayer is poured out in heathen tones, the spectacle becomes interesting, and significant of the lofty mission of the early Moravians. At that time, as well as at the present, the entire passion and aims of life were directed to reclaim the savage, and to witness the effects, upon the untamed mind, of the doctrine of salvation, couched in the fascinating imagery of Moravianism. If all the transactions of that life could be brought to view, the real history, and not the fiction of the Indian character, might be realized.

The occupation of those Indians consisted in making brooms, weaving baskets and other similar articles; and their attachment to the Brethren lasted through life, few ever forsaking it when once formed, but living, dying, and receiving interment in this place of their adoption. Many of the graves of these early converts are still visible in the cemetery, on its northern side, with their respective names chiseled on the mouldering stones. To these I would have the pilgrim bend his steps, whenever he may feel prompted, by visiting Bethlehem, to recall the thoughts and pictures of an earlier age.

Among the incidents of the time to which I am now referring, one may be culled from the archives of the church[1] at Philadelphia, which will tell, in more befitting language, what I have attempted to describe. It is the visit of the Nantikok and Shawano (Shawnee) Indians to Bethlehem, which took place in July, 1752.

"On Thursday, the twentieth of July, a messenger arrived at Bethlehem, bearing a string of wampum, and commissioned by the Nantikok and Shawano Indians to speak these words:—

"'Brother, I am near to Bethlehem, and am very glad to visit it. I am not coming to treat about any particular affairs, but in order to see you.

"'Every one is glad: the chiefs are glad, the young men are glad, the women are glad, and the children are glad.'

"As soon as this message had been received, the

---

[1] Translated for and published in the "Moravian."

Brethren Owen Rice, Horsefield, and Burnside, went to meet the Indians at the Manockisy, on the road to Gnadenhütten, taking with them some refreshments. Presently the whole company appeared on the hill, marching in fine order. The men had their guns on their shoulders, butt-end foremost; an aged chief led them, carrying a pipe of peace, adorned with ribbons. As they approached the town, they began to sing: 'I rejoice to have an opportunity of visiting the Brethren.'

"Brother Joseph (Bishop Spangenberg) met the Indians at the gate leading into Bethlehem, shook hands with the old chief and bade him welcome. He then accompanied the band on their way through town. In front of the Single Brethren's House, (the present boarding-school,) the Single Brethren and boys stood grouped together, expressing their joy at the visit. Near them were the musicians, blowing the trombones. Wherever the Indians passed, men and women came to the doors and expressed satisfaction at their arrival, until they reached Friedenshütten, (a small settlement on the other side of the Lehigh,) where, in two or three hours' time, we had built enough huts to accommodate them all decently.

"After having partaken of the refreshments provided for them, they received numerous visits from our Brethren, and then betook themselves to rest, fatigued with the excessive heat which prevailed during their journey. In the evening, the chief informed us that they had a word to say unto us, requesting us to name the time and place, when and where they might declare it.

"Friday, July twenty-one. The chiefs, together with the greater part of the Indians, assembled in our little Hall, and, after friendly salutations had been interchanged, the speaker stood up, holding a string of wampum in his hand, and spoke as follows:—

"'Brother, I am come from Gnadenhütten to Bethlehem, and will not now repeat what I said there; though with this string of wampum, I will brighten thy eyes afresh, open thy ears, wipe off thy sweat, make thy throat smooth, and thy inwards clean, as I did at Gnadenhütten; at the same time, again declaring, that we are very glad to see Bethlehem. All are glad, even the children.'

"Hereupon he presented the string of wampum, which Bishop Spangenberg received, assuring him that they were welcome, and declaring that they had seen with their own eyes, how all rejoiced at their arrival. The speaker now stood up a second time, with another string of wampum in his hand, and said: 'Brother, I come from Wajomik (Wyoming) to Gnadenhütten, from Gnadenhütten to Bethlehem, and from Bethlehem I proceeded to my quarters. I have cleared all the way with great care, taken the stones away, so that the foot dash not against them; have grubbed up all the stumps, cut off the boughs, raised the valleys, leveled the mountains, so that one cannot only go from Bethlehem to Gnadenhütten, but also from Bethlehem to Wajomik, without impediment, and from Wajomik to Bethlehem; there is nothing more in the way. I have also swept clean in Bethlehem; a person may go from Bethlehem to our quarters, and from our quarters to Bethlehem, without hinderance; the road is all as smooth and even as here in this hall.'

"When the speaker had concluded, Bishop Spangenberg took the string of wampum in his hand, and said: 'This is a weighty word, in our estimation, but very agreeable. We will speak with one another about it, and give you an answer as soon as we are prepared to do so.' Here the interview ended. This was followed by an evening service in the church, attended by nearly all the Indians, who were profoundly attentive. On the following day they received visits from the inhabitants of Bethlehem, and, on Sunday, all attended church.

"Other Indians from the Susquehanna having arrived, together with a number of the Indian Brethren and Sisters from the Gnadenhütten and Meniologamekah settlements, the whole number amounted to one hundred and thirty-six.

"In the afternoon, a baptism of an Indian woman took place, with two Sisters dressed in white; and two Brethren, standing on each side, acted as sponsors, while the Indians, seated in a circle around them, could see and hear the whole ceremony.

"On Monday, the twenty-fourth, we informed the

Indians, our answer was ready. The interview again took place in the 'little Hall.' In the centre stood a round table, covered with a red cloth. Two lighted candles stood upon it. On the one side of the table sat the chiefs, and behind them their people; on the other side, our Elders, several missionaries to the heathen, and as many Brethren and Sisters as the hall could contain. Three persons from Philadelphia were present.

"In the first place, Bishop Spangenberg arose and bade welcome to the Indians, asking them if they were ready to hear our answers. They replied, 'Gladly!' Thereupon he spoke as follows:—

"'Brother, you have come from Gnadenhütten to Bethlehem in a time of great heat; at your arrival, you brightened our eyes, wiped off our sweat, cleansed our ears, made our throats smooth, and purified our inwards with this string of wampum,' pointing to the string which they had given, and then lying on Father Nitschmann's knee.

"'You have also assured us, that it was a pleasure for your chiefs, your young men, your women, and your children, to come and visit the Brethren. We thank you for this visit. We should have cleared your eyes, wiped off your sweat, purged your ears, made smooth your throat, and your inwards clean, but found that what we did at Gnadenhütten to this end was sufficient. Your eyes were clear and your ears open before our words entered them. Nothing bad has taken hold of you; the good has had an entrance. We rejoice at your being here, and you must have seen that old and young, men and women, yea, the children, share this joy.'

"The Indian speaker then arose and repeated Bishop Spangenberg's speech, in the Nantikok language, the Indians pronouncing a hearty 'Yes!' after each sentence.

"When he had finished and taken his seat, Bishop Spangenberg stood up and answered the second word of the Indians, which referred to the second string of wampum received from them, and now lying on Father Nitschmann's knee. Pointing to it with his finger, he said:—

"'Brother, you have told us, by this string of wampum, that you have not only made the way clear in Bethlehem, but also from here to Gnadenhütten, yea, as far as Wajomik. You have raised all the valleys, leveled the hills, taken away the stumps and the stones, against which one might have dashed the foot; you have cut down the woods, so that one can see from Bethlehem to Wajomik and from Wajomik to Bethlehem, and pass to and fro without hinderance. All this is a matter of great weight and extremely agreeable to us. We will abide by your words, make frequent use of the road, so that no grass grow upon it; and if bad people throw a stone upon that way, we will carefully remove it. If the roots begin to sprout, we will grub them up again, so that the ways always remain clear. You, also, will frequently make use of it, and this will be a pleasure to us.'

"Spangenberg now delivered the belt of wampum to the speaker, who took it and repeated this address in the Nantikok language. Every sentence was received by the Indians with applause.

"The speaker having taken his seat, Spangenberg then produced the belt of wampum, given by the Six Nations to Zinzendorf,[1] ten years before, and

---

[1] The belt of wampum, here referred to, was that given to Zinzendorf, under the following circumstances, as related by Spangenberg:—

"When the Count (in 1742) set out for Tulpehokin, he encountered on his way three Sachems of the Five Nations, who had been in Philadelphia, and were now on their return home. One of these was an Onondago, one a Cayuga, and the other an Oneida chief.

"As soon as Zinzendorf understood who they were, he communicated with them, and told them that he came to them and their people with a word from the Lord, and as he brought these tidings in part himself and in part through his Brethren, he wished them to say whether they were satisfied to receive them. It was not his nor his Brethren's object to buy land of them, nor to trade with them, but only to point out the way to eternal happiness to such of them as were willing to have it shown them.

"Conrad Weiser, the provincial interpreter, explained these views to them, and added:—'This is the man whom God has sent from across the seas to the Indian, as well as the white people, in order to make them know His will to them.' He then gave them a present, after the Indian custom, to add strength to his words. The Indians received it, and then held a consultation among themselves, as they were wont to do, before one given by them to Bishop Camerhoff two years previously, at the great council of Onondago, renewing the covenant intended by the first belt; and handing these to the chiefs, they examined them very closely, and told each other what they signified.

"After these and other transactions had transpired, Brother Schlägel entered the Hall, bearing a large basket full of tobacco, which he placed at Bishop Spangenberg's feet; while Sister Schlägel, in the name of the Sisters, brought two smaller baskets filled with thread, ribbons, needles, pins, scissors, and thimbles, telling the Bishop, in a low tone of voice, that the Sisters, seeing the presents which the

---

giving answer to an embassy. After the expiration of half an hour, two of the chiefs came to the Count, and addressed him as follows:—

"'Brother, you have come a long way to us over the sea to preach to the white people and to the Indians. You did not know that we were here, and we knew nothing of you. This was done by a high hand above. Come to us, you and your Brethren, you will be made welcome. Take with you this fathom of wampum as a token that our words are the truth.'

"The belt contained one hundred and eighty pieces of wampum. In 1743 the Count gave me this belt of wampum for future use, before my intended departure for America, and when, in the course of several years, I visited Onondago, where the Five Nations were accustomed to hold their great council, they soon brought the above incident to remembrance. When we produced the belt of wampum they recognized it, counted the wampums, and knew how many had been on the strings." (*Spangenberg's Life of Zinzendorf.*)

Brethren had prepared, were anxious to make one also, and had, therefore, sent these articles. Then the Bishop again stood up, and said: 'Brother, our young people, made glad by your visit, have brought you a small present of tobacco. You have a great way home; receive this gift in love. Our women, also, have brought two baskets, full of presents for your women. A small company of our children, living not far from here, at Maguntsche,[1] having heard of your being here, resolved to bring you their morsels of bread, but fearing that it might get too dry on your journey, they have sent five bushels of meal instead, which you can divide among yourselves.'

"Thereupon, the Indians closed the interview in the following manner:—The most aged chief of the Shawnees stood up and expressed his satisfaction to his people, who responded with acclamations of joy. The most aged chief of the Nantikoks stood up and spoke in the same way to his people, who also received his words with applause. Next another chief arose, turned to us, and assured us, in the English language, that they were heartily satisfied and thankful. Finally, the speaker, who had conducted the interview on the part of the Indians, took the belts of wampum in his hand, which the Brethren had given, held them aloft, and, in a very slow pace, marched around the table. When opposite to Bishop Spangenberg, he remained standing a few minutes,

[1] Now Macungy, in Lehigh County.

and then continued his circuit, at the same time singing a short song of thanksgiving. This ceremony was followed by general applause from the Indians, and then was this whole business concluded."[1]

At that time, Bethlehem and Nazareth, ten miles apart, were kept in constant communication with each other; the forest that intervened between them was dense, and the journeyings to the latter were accompanied with difficulties. Indeed, the old chronicles tell us how the first parties going to Nazareth were preceded by axe-men to fell the trees and clear the way. When the harvests at Nazareth were ample, and laborers were wanted, Bethlehem sent its people to assist in taking off and garnering the well-laden sheaf.

The spiritual Principal of the Sisters' House at Bethlehem occasionally repaired to Nazareth to perform the duties of visitation, and among the remarkable personages who figured in those primitive times were Sister Anna Rosel and Susel von Gers-

---

[1] This visit of the two Indian tribes to Bethlehem was the result of an embassy sent to Gnadenhütten on the fifteenth of the same month, in order to make acquaintance with the Brethren, of whom they had had good reports through some of their own people. Bishop Spangenberg met them at the latter place, and the ceremonies enacted there were in nearly the same order as just related of the Bethlehem visit. Upon dismissing the party, they presented them a tanned deer-skin, to mend their children's shoes, by the way, adding to it sixty bushels of flour and eighty pounds of tobacco, which were received with expressions of joy. (See *Loskiel's History of the Moravian Missions.*)

dorf. In affairs of moment, these Sisters were called in aid, and their authority was duly submitted to in all matters of female jurisdiction.

Bethlehem being then, as it yet is, the central point of the Moravians and the seat of their ecclesiastical government in this country, all the newly-arrived emigrants and visitors from Europe directed their steps hither. During the Revolution, it, as well as Nazareth, became the refuge of American officers and soldiers, and many a company of troops stopped at these towns, and quartered over night, or for days, enjoying their hospitalities. The chivalric La Fayette, after the battle of Brandywine, was taken, wounded, to Bethlehem, where he was generously cared for, and received every attention until his recovery. The friendly Mohican, the American soldier, or the foreign officer, were alike the recipients of Moravian sympathy, and could, at all times, flee thither as to a stronghold of defence and succor.

Among the fine episodes in the history of Bethlehem, we must not disregard that of the presentation by the Sisters of the banner to Count Pulaski.[1] The memory of this event has been consecrated by Longfellow, in a poem, which, although filled with imagery entirely incongruous in its relations to the place and people whom it is designed to commemorate, is still expressive, in the finest light, of a transaction that showed, like all others, the catholic philanthropy of

[1] The banner is now in possession of the Maryland Historical Society.

the Moravian Brethren and Sisters. It was a prescribed tenet of the Moravian to submit to the ruling government, and whether the Sisters, in abetting the cause of the Revolution, acted in strict conformity with that rule, is a question we can hardly allow entrance here, as the whole incident seems to have been a matter of romance, which ought not to be marred by any prosaic considerations.

Many a former visitor to Bethlehem may yet retain some vivid recollections of an old time-worn bridge, that conducted him across the waters of the Lehigh, when approaching the town. This bridge was an uncovered structure; the wood-work had become gray with age, and as the foot-passenger loitered on its side-walk, and scanned the beauties of the stream above and below, with the Lehigh hills before him to the south, he was loath to leave such an enchanting point of view. When the coach from Philadelphia, after an hour's severe toil across the mountains, rolled into the valley, its inmates were greeted at sunset with the glowing scene before them. On the opposite side, they were pleased to recognize, once more, the antique walls of the Sister's House, the school, the imposing church, and numerous antiquated edifices, that gave character to the introductory portion of the town. The venerable bridge, with its placid waters beneath, stood ready to receive you, and having no covering to obstruct the view, as the jaded steeds plodded wearily across it, the eye was delighted with the scene it entered upon.

A quarter of a century has done much to impair that beautiful picture. Nearly all the quaintness of life and character has disappeared, and though many of the self-same structures remain that made their hold upon the imagination, new designs of architecture have, in general, supplanted the old, and destroyed the poetry of the past. The old bridge was swept away by the flood of 1841, and one of modern construction has taken its place. The woody slopes of the mountain have, to a great extent, been cleared, and the din of the railway and busy traffic mark the progress of civilization. Yet through the vista of these changes it is delightful to look back into the past; for the strong contrasts of the picture as it is, and as it was, lend additional charms to that which is gone and cannot be restored. Let us, therefore, occupy the spot a little longer, since it is the most pleasant and refreshing duty we have to perform.

As the traveler stood upon the old bridge, and dwelt upon the landscape, the waters of the Lehigh near by, and the southern mountains thrown into partial shade by the declining sun, his eye rested upon that wilderness of forest trees, covering the spot known as the "Island." Umbrageous boughs invited the rambler, and suitable provision was made for amusement and meditation; and thus the place became a constant resort for all, for the denizen as well as for him who spent the summer months at Bethlehem. Above and around the "Island," the Lehigh rushes

22

along, and the music of its waters animates the study which nature here presents. In its present aspect the "Island" varies little from its former appearance, and although it is, in some degree, shorn of attractions by the encroachment of the railway on the southern bank of the river, and the privacy of its solitude is invaded by the locomotive, yet in its native growth of forest trees it possesses an inextinguishable charm. Skiffs line the shore, and the current is stemmed by those who navigate the stream in order to approach and land upon the "Island." In the evening, as the boats glide near the pleasure-ground, music floats upon the water, and many gay and picturesque scenes, as in times of yore, delight the eye, although the living generation has allowed an earlier stage of true refinement to pass away, and has adopted most of our national modes of life, and thus put on much of the grossness of the day. The musical element which characterized all Moravian gayety, festivity, and pastime, has become diluted with national education and national associations, and as the German becomes merged in the American character, these strong traits of education and culture will become less and less visible.

Leaving the "Island" and all its scenes of mirth, of intellectual and musical recreation, of "vespers" and reunions of the innocent and happy, in times that have vanished, and realized in a greater or less degree by all those who have lived in or visited

Bethlehem, let us call up the reminiscences as well as the living performances of nocturnal music, by trio, or quartette, or sextette, in the open air. Serenades were ever a favorite employment of the Philharmonic Society, and, whether in honoring the nuptials of the newly-wedded, or breaking in upon the solemn stillness of the midnight hour in bidding welcome to some favored guest, or complimenting some esteemed musician, the Nocturne was assiduously cultivated. Many of the evening performances were executed on instruments, but most generally vocal clubs, after the manner of the Männerchöre, went the rounds, singing well-known and popular German airs. Of these compositions a number are yet preserved and sung, such as the "Chapel," by Kreutzer, (introduced by the well-known Herrmanns, a Bavarian company, who visited Bethlehem some years ago,) a quartette of unrivaled purity, harmony, and feeling, and listened to, time after time, with emotion by all who have heard it.

A general love of music was such a distinguishing feature of old Bethlehem, that the visitor was accustomed to hear on every side the sounds of the piano. Neither has the love of that fine art so far diminished as to take away this characteristic from its people. The decline has not been as much in the general devotion to music, as in the purity of taste, for as the national tone infuses itself into the German element, the fine classic musical cultivation of former times appears to be on the wane.

The old cemetery is now in the centre of the town, and spreading trees, casting their luxurious shadows over the sacred spot, invite the meditative or curious mind to seek for thought, or discover historical names among the mossy tablets. Here, at all times, parties sit and stroll about, for the Moravian respect for Christianity reigns supreme, and the pure joys of earth are not overclouded by the proximity of the grave. The Bethlehem Cemetery, no less a scene of social reunion than its German counterpart, is a common thoroughfare for all, and no compunction is felt when straying from the business paths of life across the precincts of the tomb. Here the obliging antiquary will aid us in tracing, among the almost defaced and illegible grave-stones, a number of the Indian names I have spoken of, which designate the resting-place of many of those early Christian converts, sons of the primitive forests, whom the Moravians of Lusatia found here.

> "Their names, their years, spelt by the unletter'd muse,
> The place of fame and elegy supply."

In the year 1842 the centennial celebration of the foundation of Bethlehem was held within the cemetery, by an evening service, with all the ritual accompaniments of wind instruments and vocal music; an event that will be long impressed upon the recollections of all present.

Passing along the southern walks of this enchanting burial-place, the eye rests upon a few remaining edifices that once constituted the most important part, as they now do the most striking features of Bethlehem. The Sisters' House, a grotesque pile of old gray stone, with its huge buttresses and its receding angles, still stands there, one of the few lingering monuments of the institutions I have been describing; while the more modern yet massive edifice, the church, bears also an historical air in its exterior, though founded in less marked and peculiar times than those which gave rise to the Sisters' House. This institution still, to some extent, fulfills its original design, and is the residence of a moderate number of elderly maidens, who, having sought this general asylum for all who were deprived of the advantages of a parental home, have dwelt here for a series of years. In accordance with primitive Moravian regulations, the maidens of the society were expected either to enter this abode, or to contribute their tax to its support, after the manner of the Herrnhutian and other German Sisters' Houses. These old regulations have gradually given way to modern ideas, as we are wont to call them, and life in the Moravian village, under its reformed system, assimilates to life all around it. The Sisters' House is tenanted by a solitary few—a lingering remnant of the past, who still cling to old images, and look with sorrow upon the new.

The church, always held in regard for its chaste and unassuming architecture, stands upon an elevated terrace, which confronts us in entering the town. In its interior arrangements, the Moravian rule of dividing male and female is still observed. The organ, built by Tanneberg, of Litiz, was formerly esteemed one of the best in the country; and, in its day, has sent forth its volumes of solemn tones, in the performance of church, funereal, and festal services. Within the vestry-room may be seen a small gallery of portraits by Haidt, representing the fathers of the church, missionaries, and all who were identified with the early history of the Brethren. These paintings now bear an antique look, the artist having lived more than a century ago. He was of Dutch origin, and many of his productions are carefully preserved in Bethlehem, Nazareth, and Litiz. In addition to the various portraits thus handed down to us, we also have from his pencil a number of sacred historical paintings, which may be seen in the churches of Bethlehem and Nazareth. Haidt, during the time he flourished, was, like most of the laity, employed in clerical duties.

The old fire-engine, claimed to be one of the first of its kind imported into this country, was brought from London in 1762, and is preserved as a curious relic. The original water-works, perhaps the first attempt to propel water by its own agency, having undergone some renovation, are still in operation, and faithfully perform their old duty of furnishing with an adequate supply the reservoir at the summit of the town.

Of the numerous individuals and personages who,

from time to time, presented themselves to the visitor, and excited his esteem and admiration, nearly all have passed away. Among the amusing and obliging characters who figured in the earlier part of the century, was old Father Thomas, whose worth and peculiarities will be held in remembrance by the class of visitors who were his cotemporaries. At a later period, Doctor Steckel and Doctor Green became well known as the *cicerones*, by right of appointment, and provided considerable entertainment, in the continual fund of humor and anecdote which they dispensed to the guests, whom they were charged to accompany around the village, through the school, the choir houses, church, cemetery, and along the banks of the Lehigh. The former of these employees reached a great age, and up to a very advanced period performed the duties of his office; but, as the years of his life accumulated, he was no longer able to discharge them, neither did he find in the new generations which followed in the footsteps of previous ones, as pilgrims to Bethlehem, the same cordial reception which had been awarded him. Doctor Green, rubicund in face, and cold water in principle, was for a long time believed by many to be an example of *theory versus practice.* True it is, that he originated the temperance and hydropathic doctrines, long before they had become popular in this country, but whether he himself was as abstemious as he claimed, remains among those problems which it "concerneth no man" to discuss.

His fame as a *cicerone*, dispensing fun and anecdote, and exaggeration of many objects and institutions of Bethlehem, as he presented them to the view of the strolling visitor, who was often rather an intruder than an appreciative guest, will be duly recorded among the minor recollections of the past, and as belonging to those portions of the Moravian picture presented on its mere surface.

Within later years a new cemetery has been laid out in that part of the town occupying the upper declivity of Nisky Hill. The grounds of Nisky Hill now form a pleasant resort, and from the winding paths along the romantic and precipitous bluff, we look down on the Lehigh, and on the mountains beyond, and all the intervening landscape. Its walks are among the most pleasant that Bethlehem affords, being more secluded from the associations and annoyances of business life than the more trite and well-known localities on the "Island" and along the Lehigh. It is among the greatest attractions of Nisky Hill that art has done so little, and nature so much for it; and while she is left in undisturbed possession, the trees suffered to grow into tottering age, the rocks to rest unmolested in their primitive beds, decked with moss and trailing ivy, the old and young will repair here for the opposite purposes of meditation and pleasure.

In a sequestered lane, passing up from the church, there stands a quiet and well-shaded cottage, seemingly shut out from the gay and busy portion of the town, so as to excite the attention of him who passes along by the recluseness of its aspect and the rural feeling that reigns around. Here lived for many years the venerable Heckewelder,[1] elaborating in this retirement his work on Indian life, manners, and traditions; and after a career of Christian usefulness, devotion, and self-sacrifice, here he ended his days, and was interred within the cemetery we first visited. Upon his grave are cast the shadows of the same trees that overhang those of the Indians not far off. While the mortal remains of the red men and their friend repose beneath the turf, may their spirits find happiness in a realm unknown to us!

The female boarding-school was opened to the public in 1786, and though of more recent foundation than the boys' school at Nazareth, has had under its care and parental training a very large number of young ladies from all parts of the Union, as well as from the West Indies. It has been the means of attracting many persons to Bethlehem, independent of those who come as casual visitors, and as both classes of guests have increased, the several inns have so enlarged their dimensions as to become no longer recognizable. During a long and successful period of its history, this school has established such a firm hold upon the affections of its pupils, that in their retrospect of life it has be-

[1] His daughter now resides in the Sisters' House. She was the first white woman born in what is now the State of Ohio.

come an endearing point. On the female mind, the influence of that culture, which has its seat in our schools, has been more visible than on the male youth, by the adornment it has imparted to the moral character, and that tone of quiet demeanor springing out of a three years' education there.

What the observances of a Christian culture are, and how they operate upon the formation of character, and in building up in their finest symmetrical proportions the true man or the true woman, is sufficiently explained under the heads of Education and Schools, and the Moravian Cultus.

In our system it is not assumed that merely those accomplishments should be taught which are calculated to adorn the drawing-room, as in most instances these result more from great conversational powers and vivacity of temperament than from solid education. It is there that both man and woman are performers on the great stage of artificial life, where the heart is glossed over by the fictions of society, where it delivers its poetry by an assumed medium, where nature is only admired in pictures, and where words and language originate emotion, instead of allowing it to speak through them. But in rearing the female under Moravian tutelage, all true womanly susceptibilities, wherever they exist, are brought forth and cultivated, and on her return home, the girl who has been a resident of these schools for several well-spent years, gives evidence of this cultivation in the modesty and amenity of deportment which have ever distinguished the Moravian elève of either sex. It is here presupposed, however, that the subject of discipline has been a practicable and pliant one, and in all respects adapted to the application of a system which has never yet found its equal.

In the programme of instruction some modifications have been made; the former simple plan of a series of plain studies surrendering to the growing wants of a public, on whom its support must necessarily depend. Yet, even with these innovations, the excellence of the educational principle has in no material degree deteriorated, and we may regard it as being applied to a new people in a later time, and to a country whose progress shows its new phases with every decade.

Music, as far as the faculty of a young girl reaches, has ever been assiduously taught, and when taught in its purer forms of deep and classic composition, has contributed its resistless influence to the formation of soul; but where a departure from this classic taste is allowed to prevail, the general results of music on the expanding mind must be lost. As a portion of female education in its true sense, without reference to bare accomplishment, music must be regarded as of high import, and, with reference to the female, this ground has always been taken by the Moravian educator. It seems to manifest itself in the tenderness and desires of the age, as well as the country we live in, that a high intellectual standard should form the acme of all education; but if my readers will have duly weighed the scope of the system of which I have attempted an exposition, they will find that high intellectual cultivation without emotion, and that peculiar education which is its product, will never tend to the happiness of life.

Within recent years, the Bethlehem School has made some creditable displays of musical proficiency in the performance of such productions as the "Creation," the "Glocke," Rossini's "Stabat Mater," Mendelsohn's "Elijah," and other works of the immortal masters. In the vocal execution of this music, the pupils certainly evince no small degree of advancement, and while the mind becomes refined by such pure culture as is characteristic of these works, it gains equally in the improvement such musical practice imparts.

It speaks in tones of commendation of our female schools, to remark, that when the girls of a past century grew up they sent their daughters hither, and when those in their turn departed to their homes, and reached the age and assumed the responsibilities of the worthy matron, with the glorious jewels of wedded life around them, these, too, were sent to the cherished Bethlehem to imbibe that which, in the innocence of girlhood, the mother and grandmother had enjoyed.

In former days, life in the school at Bethlehem was more recluse than it now is, for its whole tenor partook of the influences of the retired Moravian village, and was less molested by the gay spectacle witnessed during the summer months. The tutoress herself was at that time a prim Sister, her very attire bespeaking her calling and her destiny. In that undisturbed mode of life and education, and the absence of all the attractions of listless amusement and fashion, the results of Moravian culture were more distinctly visible than they now are, and, as it is my office to chronicle the past, rather than to panegyrize the present, I cannot refrain from wishing that that part might be restored. As the picture of that day, when the genuine type of the Moravian Sister is held up to view, becomes more dim, its poetic effect upon us increases, and, like all things appertaining to the imagination, mellows in the distance.

The Sisters' and Widows' Houses still preserve their primitive interior arrangements, and we find the oaken staircases, the flagged pavements, the small windows, and the large dwelling-rooms in the former, which were once occupied by companies of four Sisters, each sitting in her allotted corner. The low ceilings of the Widows' House, the broad oaken stairs, and the solid masonry of the walls, all speak of the past, when architecture looked forward to endurance and strength, rather than, as now, to beauty and the mere purposes of the day.

Bethlehem has been sought by the superannuated as the resting-place and the solace of declining life. It is the "Mecca" to which all those who have been employed in the service of the Moravian cause, either as pastors at home or missionaries abroad, direct their steps. In its cemetery may be found the names of many who had fulfilled the duties of the Moravian clergyman's life, labored in a long and arduous campaign of evangelical service, toiled amid the needs of poverty and the passions of humanity, living on the scanty pittance of many of our small village congregations, then risen to posts of comparative eminence in their sphere, and, finally, received an earthly reward by being allowed their humble portion and the enjoyment of quiet, sweetened by social happiness, in this place. This reunion of the old always seemed to strengthen the bonds of their attachment to Bethlehem, and even constituted a society within itself. The circumstances of their residing here in such numbers gave a tone to the moral and religious character of the place, and more especially during its isolated condition, when it was an exclusive community. Since the law of exclusion has been laid aside, and a promiscuous population has been invited to come and dwell here, society has become more diluted, and the retired missionary is no longer a prominent object.

Bethlehem has been visited by large numbers of our citizens, as well as by many foreigners of distinction, and has been the abiding-place of the invalid, or of those who desire tranquil leisure during the warm summer and the autumnal months. The musical virtuoso frequently comes hither to hear and be heard, and finds the society around him, particularly if he be a German, congenial and appreciative. Standing on the borders of a picturesque and romantic stream, in the midst of a captivating landscape, confronted by mountains, and with a salubrious air coming down the long valley that stretches to the west, it charms alike the visitor and the resident. A mixed society has thus sprung up, which no longer leaves the Moravian so distinctly marked as before, nor is the town as striking and sedate in aspect. Many of the old land-marks, however, together with the remnants of social life which the memory delights to dwell upon, are yet to be traced, and tell us that something still remains of the old Moravian town. Scarcely a year elapses without a number of the retired apostles of the church, or some aged inhabitant who had grown up and was nurtured in a fondness for the beautiful simplicity of the older school, passing from off the scene. All such, while they live, cling to the institutions in which they were cradled, and are loath to exchange the associations of German life, its warmth and its festivities, for the modern style of American modes and practices. But as this generation passes away, a new stage of men and things supervenes, receiving its impress from "young America," and looking forward to a world of hopes, based upon the materialism and progress of the age in which we figure. The spiritual life of Moravianism, founding its hopes and aspirations in a world of future perfection, and its rewards not in the dross of life, but in the jeweled crown of eternity, is fast merging into American forms of thought and action, and casting off its German parentage and relationship. Yet, notwithstanding this admixture of a modern and national element, the summer months may be pleasantly whiled away in and around Bethlehem, for the seductions of nature here are great, either in the drive to Allentown, to "Bauer's Rock," a craggy eminence to the southwest, upon the loftiest part of the Lehigh range, and commanding a wide-extended view, along the southern banks of the stream, toward Hellertown, or Freemansburg, or northwardly toward Bath or Nazareth. This whole region is so fertile and romantic, and, in its champaign aspects, so picturesque, that the seeker of rural enjoyment can find abundant solace in all he sees in these precincts, and in the excursions that are within range.

Notwithstanding the innovations of the mechanical arts and of commerce upon the poetical beauties of the Lehigh, whose banks have been trodden, time after time, by the serious and the gay, nature is beautiful yet, and sufficient remains of the native forest trees, with the clear sparkling waters of the old Indian stream beneath them, to gladden the imagination and soothe the heart of the stricken in years, as he once more seeks his wonted resting-place.

A commercial age is apt to lay aside the instincts that direct themselves to the pure and the beautiful in nature, and those equally chaste affections which linger among the decaying emblems and images of the past,—exchanging them for the gilded toys of a later school of taste and design, in which a higher spirituality is but feebly developed. Wherever this latter quality clings to the events and structures of the olden time, I would fain see its remembrance preserved and held sacred, and some monumental tribute bestowed upon it as its only and its highest temporal recompense.

XIV.

MUSIC AT BETHLEHEM AND NAZARETH.

AFTER offering the sketch of the interview with the Nantikok and Shawano Indians within the "Little Hall," as it was then called, I will introduce the reader into the same apartment under a different appropriation. This venerable chapel occupies the upper portion of the building adjoining the Sisters' House, the entrance to which is found by ascending a small flight of wooden steps, and thence by an ancient and well-worn staircase with its oaken balustrade.

Here music in its higher forms might often have been heard. To the select auditory that delighted to gather here, concerts were given by an orchestra of amateur musicians, aided by the voices of the Sisters, who joined in the Euterpean relaxation, and in which all ages united, from the girl of sixteen to the matron, whose voice remained vigorous until the frame decayed.

In these evening concerts the well-filled chapel generally testified an appreciative audience, where all came to listen, enjoy, and discuss the merits of the performance, at the close of which no applause was ever offered, for the general feeling of quiet satisfaction that prevailed was understood, and was of itself a sufficient guaranty for the required approbation. In these pleasant soirées the entertainment was always of a genial character, and nothing offensive to good taste was ever admitted to mar the sanctity of the old chapel.

Of the veteran virtuosi who still dwell in Bethlehem, it is gratifying to find many who, year after year, repaired to that old music hall, for the greater part of the present century, and kept alive, by their devotion to the cause of the divine art, the taste of the community for the best works of the tone-masters. Most of these amateurs were engaged in the ordinary avocations of an industrious life, and many left their work-benches, at the close of day, to take up in the evening the violin, the 'cello, the flute, or the contra-bass. A professed musician was seldom seen here, except when giving an exhibition for his personal benefit. This love of music was inherent in the Moravian, and was, along with the whole system of religious culture, introduced from Europe.

Although the chapel was the scene of regular evening entertainments, given by the Philharmonic Association, generally throughout the winter and sometimes in the summer months, during an influx of visitors, the most charming of them all was that on the anniversary of Whitmonday, called the

Musical Festival. Upon entering the Little Hall, we beheld the joyous evergreen, woven into the accustomed wreath, with which the walls were tastefully draped. Grunewald, the artist, lent his aid to animate the occasion, by furnishing pictorial images of Apollo, and his votaries Beethoven and Mozart. This combination of the sister arts, united with the services of the ladies, who formed the wreaths and garlands and fashioned the nosegays of the early summer flowers, lent to the scene an air of poetical interest and naïve enjoyment. The auditory of an earlier day looked to musical performances as a portion of life's sustenance, and combined them with the pastimes and vacant hours that found their way among the sterner duties of a commonplace reality. These simple decorations, the truest emblems of the spirit and design of the Festival, suggested at a period of the year when nature begins to expand to both eye and ear, appealed with wondrous effect, to the annual guest, of the welcome musical banquet.

This Festival had become of such old standing, that it was regarded as a permanent institution, and if aught transpired to hinder its celebration, a cloud of disappointment seemed to cast its shadows over the public mind. The entertainment lasted the whole day, and to the chronicler of medieval Bethlehem, it forms a bright point to look back upon. In addition to a well-selected programme, an oratorio was usually presented to the dilettanti, and among all these compositions the selections from Haydn and Mozart were ever the favorites. The virtuosi of Bethlehem claim the honor of having first introduced to the notice of an American public Haydn's "Creation," and, although it made its first appearance in Philadelphia, the *score* was furnished by them to Mr. Hupfeldt, who succeeded in bringing it out before a Philadelphia audience.

The merit of having transplanted this production of Haydn from Germany into America was no small one, as it is probably the most chaste work of vocal melody the tone-master has ever produced, and appeals by its purity of thought and its idyllic gentleness to the sense of our common humanity. Haydn, indeed, composed for all countries and all ages, and his melody never fades from the musical vision; hence his master-piece was warmly studied among us, and his beauties were appreciated, alone at the piano, in the church choral music, or in the public concert.

A venerable and esteemed citizen of Bethlehem long continued to be the regular performer of Adam, in the duet of Adam and Eve, while the latter character was usually personified by a young maiden. The youthful Eve never flourished long upon the musical stage, for as she ripened into womanhood the common destiny of life stole her away, giving place to another, and she again in her turn to yet another. Many, therefore, were the maidens, who, in their short-lived career of the Moravian prima donna of the "Little Hall," sung Eve, yet Weiss outlived them all; and it is but recently we have had the pleasure of seeing him stand up and perform his part, with his deep sonorous voice and well-studied delivery, such as he was ever wont to display in the execution of parts appropriated to him. Since its first introduction, which was thirty-three years ago, the public have been favored with this work of Haydn nearly every year, and there is no portion of its popular choruses that is not familiar to all who have attended the Bethlehem concerts of secular and sacred music.

Other oratorios have met with similar success, and were for a long time diligently rehearsed by the Philharmonic Association. Among these may be named the "Seasons," by Haydn, a work wherein the pastoral conceptions of the composer speak through the same language of tone that gives itself utterance in the rural imagery of the "Creation," and among many was as much cherished as the "Creation" itself. Aside of this, may be named Schiller's "Glocke," performed in German, and set to music by Romberg. In the "Glocke" we find that rare excellence of the most exquisite and moral poetry wedded to choice melody. These merits contributed to make it an old favorite, as the poem is one of the classic productions of the German anthology, and stands almost unrivaled for its sincerity and pathos. To these may be added the "Seven Sleepers," and numerous other minor selections from Mendelsohn, Mozart, Beethoven, Rossini, and others of the German and Italian schools.

Occasionally, a musical celebrity would stray hither, to hear and be heard;. the atmosphere around him was musical, and the inducements to while away a month irresistible. Of such the "Bavarian Minstrels," whom I have noticed in the preceding sketch, will long be remembered, as their vocal performances were the inspiration of a perfect harmony of feeling, and their skillful expression displayed a mastery in the art of tone. At a later period, Knoop's achievements on the violincello left indelible impressions behind, and no one either before or after him could deliver such exquisite combination of tone-thought on that most expressive of all instruments.

In the chapel of Nazareth Hall, the teachers and citizens were wont to assemble in the evenings, and rehearse many of the symphonies of Haydn and other composers, together with an excellent programme of chamber music, in trios, quartettes and quintettes, and when engaged in the symphony, they employed as full an orchestra as they could muster. Each virtuoso, on his own favorite instrument, from the violincello to the kettle-drum, gave his whole soul to the subject, and if the performers, as a *tout-ensemble*, did not arrive at the proficiency of professed artists, they at least displayed the feeling, which is one of the first requirements of music, and often redeems the deficiencies of skill.

A favorite of these genial Haydn symphonies was the "Farewell," which was signalized by the successive disappearance of the lights. One performer after another, each as he closed his part, successively extinguished his taper, the music grew fainter, the sounds fell gradually into a pensive *andante*, another taper was extinguished, until the last survivor of that gay symphony was left alone, playing in his solitary position; and as the notes of his violin melted insensibly into feebler tones, and died away, he seemed, in extinguishing his own taper, to close the scene, and to drop the curtain on some fine dramatic act.

As regards the other Moravian villages, music was industriously studied, although concert and chamber music were more successful in Bethlehem and Nazareth than elsewhere, for here there was a constant accession of proficients from Europe, who kept the flame alive, as the German Moravian student was, with rare exception, well trained in the art. Within recent years, as previously observed, the female Boarding-school at Bethlehem has taken up the cause of vocal music, performing the works of Haydn, Romberg, Mendelsohn, Rossini, and even Beethoven, in a very creditable style of execution and expression.

On the evening previous to the "Public Exhibition," in June, the large church is used for an entertainment, being lighted with gas, in modern contrast with the obscure candles of the old chapel. An ample stage, adorned with arches of evergreen festoons, is thrown up, sufficient for the accommodation of nearly two hundred young ladies and a few gentlemen, who represent the bass and tenor parts. Throwing aside the primness of a former time, the girls are attired in the costume of the day, and the effect upon the large audience that sit before them is highly pleasing, as, in a glorious chorus of the "Creation," they all rise up beneath a flood of light that is shed upon them.

In speaking of music as a past or declining feature in the Moravian character in America, the fact must not be overlooked that this remark applies only to certain forms. The cultivation of the voice and proficiency on the piano are as great as ever, and perhaps they are carried to a higher degree of perfection than hitherto; it is only in orchestral and chamber music that we can say that public taste has arrived at a turning point. As long as the Philharmonic Society of Bethlehem and the old Concert Hall flourished, and were upheld by a kind of traditional veneration for the music in which every one had been reared from childhood, the German school of composition was rigidly adhered to; but now the modern Italian school has crept in, and receives that common admiration for its transient beauty, which it finds all over the world, wherever man is susceptible of the influence of modulated tone. Selections from it are usually produced by the Sextette Club, or they become familiar to the ears of the piano pupil, through the numerous popular musical publications that flood the country.

The most characteristic of all music among the Moravians is that of the trombone, played usually in the open air, on the belfry, in the graveyard, at the church-door, and, at New Year's eve, in the orchestra. Here the Moravian hymn is drawn out with wonderful expression, and in rendering its harmonies on these pensive wind instruments, we catch all its beauties in their fullest force. The trombones are generally played in quartette, and when the chorales are correctly executed by guiding the crescendo to its proper point, and imparting to the air its finest shades of meaning, the out-door impressions are deep and abiding. Many of these well-known chorales are very ancient, but their exquisite tone combinations never permit them to tire upon the cultivated ear, the long vibratory notes blending in beautiful accord when passing out of the sombre instrument. In their musical history of a past century the trombone has imparted solemnity to the opening and close of every anniversary; the quartette, with their thrilling tones, adding poetry to the transactions of life, as well as to the religious cultus.

The Sextette Club, already alluded to, has been instituted by the young men of Bethlehem, who perform on the cornet, and the music, although of a different school of composition from that of the trombone, is a great acquisition to out-door recreation and entertainment. The Sextette not only enliven many a public occasion with choice and popular melodies, selected from the modern opera, but they even produce, with effect, the classic compositions of the great masters; and their instruments, with that remarkable ductility of sound that distinguishes them, adapt themselves to compositions of a solemn cast. On the waters of the Lehigh, or in the street, when the evening has subsided into the deep quiet of night, the Sextette is often heard and listened to with fixed enjoyment. Within the last few years the Sextette Club has added greatly to the day's happiness of a Nazareth Reunion. Early in the morning a coach is seen entering the town, filled with the members of the club, who perform some chosen air as they arrive at the place where the old pupils are assembled. They precede the procession to the Hall, play in the church as introductory to the address; play at the supper table, where mirth and good humor run high; and, finally, crown the closing scene of leave-taking in the square by some stirring strain that softly dies away as the last of the Reunionists retreat from the scene.

If the cultivation of music has never reached that artistic perfection of which it is susceptible, when made an engrossing pursuit, it has been so generally introduced into all the movements of social life that its aim and influences have been carried out to their fullest extent. When music has been so fully incorporated with every form of a people's life, leading them along by its irresistible power over the heart and soul, and making them familiar with its tone-visions—visions of a far higher order than all the materialistic associations of earth—we must conclude that it has left some marked results upon their character. In the ordinary course of a callous existence, tone-thoughts always awaken new feelings, and by the accessory of song or instrumental music the most ordinary event becomes a matter of poesy. Thus we have seen that the Birth-day celebration was often enlivened by a greeting from a musical chorus; a marriage-feast was serenaded in the evening; the days of public rejoicing were ushered in by sweet sounds.

We have seen, too, in the whole history of the religious cultus, that music ever presided: it cheered every festival, it held all ascetism at a distance, it warmed the whole religious life, it filled every observance with spirituality and made every ritual a matter of deep emotion, it attained that paramount object of making religion an enjoyment. It would be superfluous to offer a defence of music, in its fraternity with a religious cultus, as the world has never yet seen a form of Christianity of which the external worship was not combined with some rhythmical form or musical demonstration. A Christian cultus has often appeared wherein the indications of a musical emotion are scarcely descernible, but even among communities who endeavor to stifle this instinct of human nature the elementary conditions of the art are unconsciously manifested. The very first suggestions that originate modulated melody arise from the pulsations of the human heart, and as these pulsations are impressible in any individual, so the primary musical element is found in every human being.

In order to adapt music to the necessities of real life its early study should be regarded as an essential of education, and hence we have seen that a large portion of the Moravian's academic years were occupied in the simple exercises of the art. Reared from an infantile age among the beautiful associations of tone, thoughts clothed in the language of melody became the companions of each individual's private meditations. The *motive* of an air is never lost in the memory, the sacred hymn learned in youth dies only with the mind itself, and hence, as a portion of a religious cultus, its cultivation should never be lost sight of.

XV.

THE MISSIONARY ENTERPRISE.

It might be supposed that among a people living in small communities of three to five hundred souls, and instituting for themselves a peculiar life of thought and worship, all those forms of religious and educational culture, at which we have just glanced, should have some ulterior and useful aims to fulfill, not only in relation to themselves, but to others without the pale of their society. As we have seen it become their mission, in the maturity of their history, to educate the civilized, so too it became equally important to evangelize the uncivilized portions of the earth.

The life of the Moravian at home, though quiet, industrious, and unpretending, not only exhibited good results within itself, by its peculiar practices and limited worldly aspirations, but diffused its influences abroad in the vast scale of its missionary labors. These may be termed vast, when we consider the small means, both as to wealth and numbers, of the people who sent forth the ardent and undaunted heralds of Christian salvation. It may be said that one, as much as the other, of these enterprises, gave a certain share of celebrity to the Moravians, occupying, as they do, more than a century and a quarter of time, and having the whole civilized and uncivilized world for their theatre of action. In this manner, a promiscuous public, without reference to sect, have formed their acquaintance by supporting their schools, and thus mixing with them and studying their music and rituals; while the missionary, extending his labors and researches in fields never previously trodden or ventured upon by other pioneers, sent his modest fame abroad by the singular, and apparently miraculous, preservation he met with in endeavoring to gain over the aboriginal of every clime and of the most aggressive species of humanity.

By many it is deemed a questionable philanthropy to leave the work of Christian truth undone and neglected at home, and carry the tidings it proclaims into distant regions, where idolatry has so firm a foothold as to render man unimpressible to purely spiritual doctrines and unsusceptible of abstract ideas regarding the divine and the holy. Yet the Moravians, while they have attended to this field at home, and to the dissemination of the truth, as they view it, among the villages and the cities of Europe and America, independent of their own congregations, by maintaining a regular corps of home missionaries have, at the same time, always regarded their special mission to be the propagation of the gospel among the heathen.

It is the peculiar attribute of Moravian Christianity to bring before the mind the personality of Christ, and to represent the spectacle of his life, sufferings, and death, in those palpable forms that render him constantly visible to the infantile and unsophisticated candidate for hope, peace, and salvation. The Moravian lyric is replete with terminology, expressive of this personality, and so much so, that in the older sacred poetry of the church the tendency was rather overdrawn, and the expressions of the suffering Christ led to vague and extreme meanings, which were only interpretable by the Moravians themselves. Yet, under all this symbolism, the ground-work of a beautiful faith lay concealed, and in appealing to the rude but susceptible heart of the untamed man, the faith of the cross was educed in its abstract sense from the visible representation of God in the human form, and the endowment of this same form with all the love and sympathies of man himself.

In the hymn that was taught the Indian, the same phraseology was always introduced, and thus his untutored heart softened under the benign influence of Moravian worship.[1] In some instances, the work of

[1] Of the nature and reception of the doctrines taught, Loretz says: "It is no matter of surprise that the Brethren should remain steadfast in their adherence to the fundamental truths of Christianity, the knowledge of Christ, and the knowledge of human conception. The Scriptures teach them, and experience among all mankind confirms them, and

the missionary was abandoned, after one or more years of persevering effort, but these futile attempts were

---

this confirmation has received additional weight from the wide intercourse of the Brethren with so many moral and immoral classes of mankind, enabling them to discover the great uniformity of the one leading idea amid the greatest disparity of races.

"Civil institutions, education, climate, and food, give rise to as great a diversity among nations as that which exists among the individuals of a single people; yet it is clear that one character is discernible in our whole race; that man has been created for one common destiny; that his capacity for knowledge and emotion, although differing in degree, is universal, and hence, that the declarations of Holy Writ regarding the natural man are truth. To exemplify this, it is apparent to all men that there is a God. We have met with Greenlanders, in a perfect state of nature, who had not a single word in their language expressive of the Deity, but after their conversion they have acknowledged that in silent, thoughtful hours, when they contemplated the sea, the mountains, the heavens, and other objects of creation, a mighty thought seized them that all this must be the work of some great being.

"It is evident, too, that in every man there exists a consciousness of moral or immoral conduct,—whether this be an innate or an acquired conception is immaterial.

"The conscience accuses; there are thoughts of reproof and thoughts that justify us, and, under all grades of intelligence, there are actions which are accompanied with the conviction of right and wrong. A moral feeling underlies the conviction that, after death, we shall be rewarded or punished for our actions. This same feeling is found pervading the most savage tribes, instructing them that the Deity must be pleased, let their general knowledge be ever so circumscribed.

mostly in climes very distant and scarcely accessible, and the journeying to them extremely hazardous and expensive. Thus he sought Lapland in 1734, and the Samoyedes in 1737, and in 1739, had already penetrated Palestine and Ethiopia; these, with Algiers, Ceylon, China, Persia, the East Indies, and the mountains of the Caucasus, are all

---

Sin, therefore, lays its burden upon every one, on the uncivilized as well as the moral and refined.

"Nearly all nations have their sorcerers or their jugglers, who administer various forms of purification in order to cleanse them of moral evil, and appease their God. Others have their sacrifices to conciliate their idols and render them propitious. All this coincides with the Scripture, where it dwells upon the corruption of man and the necessity of a reconciliation with God.

"The more intimately we have become acquainted with heathen nations the more fully have we discovered that the Greenlander, the Negro, the Hottentot, the Indian, the moral or the immoral individual, the weak and the strong minded, have all had the same experience in the work of conversion.

"Further evidence in favor of this is seen in the experience of thousands among other sects, whatever may have been their nation, their caste, education, or capacities; they may have been scattered over various portions of the earth and dwelt far from each other, still, on nearer examination, it will be found that their inner history was the same, that under the greatest diversity of temperament, but one common want was felt, and but one means of assuaging it was found. And thus the truth of the doctrine of Jesus and his apostles has been established among the Brethren, and proved the never-failing source of consolation and of strength." (*Ratio Disciplinæ Unit. Frat.*)

abandoned mission-grounds, as well as those in Guinea, among the Calmucks, in Abyssinia and Tranquebar. Although the Brethren were obliged to relinquish them, it was not without long-continued effort, extending in some places to half a century, and among the Calmucks to eighty years. Their existing missions still take in an extensive range, and include Surinam, the Mosquito coast, the English and Danish West Indies, the Indian territories of our great West, and of Canada, Labrador, and Greenland. In the eastern hemisphere they flourish at the Cape of Good Hope, Australia, (which has been temporarily relinquished, but bids fair to be revived,) and, at this moment, two enterprising and undaunted missionaries are exploring Thibet, Mongolia, and the Himalaya regions.

The earliest mission was undertaken in 1732, by Leonhard Dober and David Nitschmann, the one a potter, the other a carpenter, who proceeded to St. Thomas, West Indies, and broke the first ground there.

Although the primitive missionary conception in the mind of Zinzendorf had its birth in the "Senfkorn Order," at school, in common with De Watteville, his first practical idea on the subject appears to have occurred to him on a visit to Copenhagen in the year previous to the departure of the two first missionaries. While studying there, he made acquaintance with the Royal Master of the Horse, the Count of Laurwig, whose attendant was a negro slave of the Danish West Indies. The Count conversed with the negro, who described the spiritually destitute condition of his fellow-slaves in the island, as well as the longing his own sister had shown for a knowledge of the true God. There, too, he learned that the Danish missions in Greenland were abandoned, and then became warmed with the thought that an extensive field lay open for the operations of the revived church of the Brethren, by its engaging in the work of missions to those distant countries, the West Indies and Greenland. The Count returned to Herrnhut, and his reception was signalized by the warmest demonstrations of feeling on the part of the congregation, who went out to meet him and to congratulate him on his safe arrival. They knew nothing of the new schemes that had resulted from his visit to Denmark, and received with joy and surprise the first suggestions made to them by Zinzendorf. There were many ardent minds among them, who embraced a proposition to go forthwith to the West Indies, and among these were Leonhard Dober and Tobias Leopold; and, on hearing the disclosures in regard to the Greenland Danish mission, Matthias Stach came forward and offered his services in that field.

A year passed away before any action was taken on these deliberations, when Dober, the first-named individual, set out from Herrnhut, choosing Nitschmann for his companion, as the latter had formed an attachment to the negro slave of Count Laurwig. In the evening before their departure on this weighty errand, a meeting was held in Herrnhut, in which every one singly bestowed his blessing upon the two apostles, in the form of a verse; and more than one hundred verses were thus sung, and then handed to the two devoted Brethren as keepsakes.

In the same evening the Count conferred with Leonhard Dober on the duties and importance of the charge assigned him, and early in the morning, he accompanied both as far as Bautzen. Laying his hand upon the head of Dober, he imparted his benediction, and his instructions were embraced in the comprehensive command of "following in all things the spirit of Christ." He then gave them each a ducat, which, together with the sum of three dollars they each had on starting, formed their entire outfit. Then proceeding on foot along the way leading through Wernigerode, Brunswick, and Hamburg, they traveled to Copenhagen.[1]

This event was coeval with the earliest stage of the society, and a beginning having been made in St. Thomas, the Moravian settlements soon spread throughout the Danish and English islands, where they have flourished up to the present day.

With the exception of a few English and American Brethren, the great body of the missionaries are

---

[1] Croeger's Brüdergeschichte.

German; and as these die, or retire from service, their places are replenished from the mother country. In the various islands the missionary life may be exhibited in its most engaging character.

The treatment of the colored race in these tropical isles, and their induction into the doctrines, forms, and observances of the Moravian worship, are characterized by the same process by which all the semi-civilized races are led into it; but the negro himself, regarded in a social light, is considerably in advance of the converted Indian. A strong feature of the West Indian congregation is the rule, everywhere observed, of the confidential "Speaking," which is a monthly custom, and at the appointed times hundreds are seen repairing to the mission house for this purpose.

The sacraments, festivals, and Christmas and Easter solemnities, the order of interments, are all in conformity with the customs of Herrnhut, and in every island where Moravianism has taken root, the poor negro has found a sympathizing friend in the Brethren, who would not relinquish this destiny for any other that is likely to await them on earth. The humble mission house and its chapel often stand upon picturesque and pleasant locations, where the beauties of the tropical landscape abound. Climate, soil, and the mode of tillage, are such as we find beneath a vertical sun, and life partakes of those influences on health and mind that are peculiar to all Southern regions.

In the Danish islands, industry is essential to the well-being of the missionary; but in the English islands he is more exempt from manual labor, and enjoys a more placid existence.

Many places of residence are interesting spots, and the access to them is across a surface of country that resembles a garden in fertility. The most luxurious foliage and the most delicious fragrance of fruit and flowers assail the senses, and make the visitor conscious of his entrance into a land of paradisaical enjoyment. The palm and the cocoanut trees rise up in lofty magnificence around, while the superabundant fruits of the lemon and orange, filling the air with their aroma, lie untasted on the ground. The hedges are clothed in the blossom of the blooming aloe, while the cabbage-palms adorn the roadside, and lend their shadows to the traveler's relief. Among the rocks is seen growing the enormous cactus, and descending to the sea-shore, the ocean view adds to the romantic interest of the whole natural scene. To give a more perfect picture of these islands, I subjoin the following description of the visit to St. John by Breutel and Haüser:—

"On landing, we discovered at a distance some persons waiting for us; these were the Brethren Schmitz, Meyer, and Ziock. They had been joined by the chief magistrate of St. John, Mr. Brahde, who pressed us all, in the most friendly manner, to breakfast at his house, situated near the shore.

"Having spent a few hours at this hospitable mansion, we all mounted the horses, prepared for our journey to Bethany; for on this rocky island no vehicles are to be met with.

"Our caravan, consisting of seven riders and several negroes leading the horses of the Sisters and conveying our luggage, had something oriental in its appearance.

"We proceeded pretty slowly up the mountain, on the top of which, five hundred or six hundred feet high, the missionary station of Bethany is situated. It is hardly possible to conceive a more splendid prospect than that on the road over the Coral Mountains. Here a sequestered vale, with a cool, inviting grove of palms; there a neat plantation, the negro-houses of which peep through the enormous leaves of the Paradise fig-tree or of the banana. Here a herd of cattle feeding on luxuriant pastures; there a view of the ocean, with numberless rocks, surrounding the island.

"Sometimes the bridle-path leads along the summit of the mountain, so that we looked down on both sides, as from the ridge of a roof, upon the island and the sea, and could plainly discover Tortola and St. Croix. Now and then we met with a breadfruit-tree or a wild fig-tree, whose airy roots hanging down from its branches like ropes and thread, festooned themselves on the ground.

"Farther on, as we ascended higher, the road was sometimes covered over like an arbor, and from the dark-green foliage descended the amaranthine, with its red bell-shaped flowers, like a garland. The air on the top of the mountains is always pleasantly cool, owing to the sea-breezes. The forests on every side swell out in luxuriant grandeur, but they are not rendered vocal, as in our native country, by the warbling of birds; for the small number of the feathered tribe found here are totally destitute of this pleasing gift of nature."

In these regions a perpetual summer reigns, and although the chilliness of a West Indian winter is felt, still nature continues to hold her verdure, and the flowers to bloom. To this land of the sun the early missionary of 1732 was tempted to go, to seek out the forlorn negro, whose nature, though not as free and savage as the aboriginal, had never yet been illumined by any ray of Divine light.

Among this dark race the efforts of the Moravians were more successful than among any other people, and in all the islands where the earliest missions were established during the last century, they now count their numbers by tens of thousands.[1]

Early in the year 1733, three missionaries, Matthias and Christian Stach, and Christian David, set out for Greenland, and under the greatest difficulties

[1] The total number of Moravian missions throughout the globe, in 1857, was seventy, superintended by three hundred missionaries. The whole number of persons under instruction, in all the mission fields, about seventy-three thousand.

commenced the building of New Herrnhut.[1] Like the introduction of a Moravian gospel to the fairer climes of the tropics, the tale of the first missionary efforts, in Greenland and Labrador, was fearful and discouraging in the extreme; and it was not until after repeated efforts, the arrival of other Brethren, and a long endurance of suffering, privation, toil, and disease, that a foothold was gained. On the shores of this winter-bound and desolate country, four stations still exist, and the hardy Greenlander, having submitted to the missionary's teachings, becomes a consistent disciple of the glad tidings of the gospel. What renders the work among those distant and bleak countries so remarkable, is the fact of its having been undertaken and executed by two or three individuals at a time, with little pecuniary aid. These men resorted to manual labor to support themselves, and by their own exertions supplied the necessaries of life. So destitute were they of all the materials for building, that, at Lichtenfels, in 1758, they had recourse to the floating timber of wrecked vessels, which were occasionally washed on the shore. The small bark, named the "Harmony," braving the tempests and battling with the icebergs, arrives yearly from Europe, and has now performed its eightieth voyage.[2]

---

[1] Christian David made two subsequent voyages to Greenland, and erected two houses there with his own hands.

[2] No vessel that ever crossed the ocean has had a more remarkable history than this little messenger of peace, which,

But here the picture of nature is in striking contrast with that of the tropics, where we find the first seat of the Moravian missions. The supplies of the

though consisting of different structures, has borne the general name of the "Harmony."

The first ship was purchased for the purposes of the Labrador mission, in the year 1770, after its establishment had been decided upon at the Marienborn Synod. This little craft was called the "Jersey packet," and was a mere shallop of eighty tons burden!

A small company of ten Brethren, under the conduct of Haven and Drachart, arrived in Labrador in July, and having opened a friendly correspondence with the natives, the Esquimaux, returned home in safety. In the following year, a larger vessel was purchased in London, and was named the "Amity." Led by the two above-named Brethren, fourteen more individuals set sail in it, and, after a dangerous voyage, in which they encountered icebergs and fell in among the rocky coasts, landed in Labrador, and founded Nain. After "Amity," several other vessels were made use of, until the present brig, of two hundred and thirty tons, was erected at Yarmouth, under the superintendence of Captain Taylor. It is built with a prow of double timbers, and provided with an ice-breaker, in order to resist all the obstacles of the Northern seas, and is withal a good sailer.

Eighty-eight years have elapsed since these regular voyages commenced, and in all that time, and throughout the adventurous scenes necessarily encountered, no disaster to ship or crew has ever taken place.

In 1778 it fell into the hands of a French privateer, but was soon after set at liberty, by the influence of Bishop Hutton, who appealed to the French minister of marine service. In the year 1803, on its return from Labrador, it was twice pursued by a French frigate, but the darkness of the night needful requirements of life are sparse and dearly bought. For only four months in the year does summer hold its feeble sway, and the little grass that is gathered for hay is collected, in small and scattered patches, on the mountain-side. The chase is the profession of the Greenlander, as well as the Esquimaux, who pursue the reindeer on the hills, and lie in wait for the seal by the sea-shore, or skim along the surface of the wave in the light kayak, or boat of skins. Dreary as this existence may seem to us, who belong to a latitude which is especially designed for man, the missionary continues to dwell there and pursue the work that first attracted him thither. Among those ice-clad hills, and from the lips of these dwarf specimens of humanity clothed in the wild raiment of the reindeer and seal, the Moravian hymn may be heard, and the same tones ascending heavenward, that issue from the gladdened hearts of the negroes on the West Indian plantation. Christmas and Easter are here solemnized as well as at Bethlehem and Nazareth; and although the paraphernalia of the hemlock-wreath, the full-choir music, and illuminated inscriptions, are wanting to give life to the scene, yet the same spiritual motive underlies their cheerful yet simple ceremonies.

The missionary of Okak, on the coast of Labra-

---

enabled its captain to escape. The remarkable and providential preservation of the little ship, during nearly a whole century, has enabled the Brethren to keep up an uninterrupted communication with those arctic regions.

dor, living upon a solitary island, situated in an inlet, writes that he has endured his arctic life for twenty-five years. He says that his congregation, comprising three hundred and six souls, are only found at home during autumn and winter, the rest of their time being employed in hunting the seal and reindeer. When at home, they have their divine service and school every day. When the bell rings, the whole village is seen to emerge from their huts of turf, and move in long lines to church and school. The organ is played alternately by two Esquimaux Brethren, and, on festivals, anthems are sung, with a violin and flute accompaniment. The whole worldly fortune of these people consists in the reindeer and seal; if the chase has been fortunate, they are in the possession of all they desire, and spend the winter at home amid the rituals and hymns of Herrnhut. When they disperse, throughout the summer, in quest of game, wandering perhaps two hundred miles, on their dog-sleds, beyond their homes, they sometimes escape from spiritual life, and the missionary finds it his duty to recall them to his fold, whence they had strayed too long.

The first missionary to South Africa was George Schmidt, who, in 1737, landed at Cape Town, and settled at Bavianskloof, in the interior of the country. After remaining here for eight years he was obliged to suspend the work, through the opposition of the Dutch clergy, and he returned to Germany. On the spot where he first preached to the Hottentots, he planted a pear-tree. This tree grew up, and in 1792, fifty years afterwards, meetings were held beneath its shade. The venerable Archivist of Herrnhut, who takes a pleasure in producing all remarkable reminiscences of missionary life, still shows the identical pears, gathered from Schmidt's tree.

After this long interval of time, three mechanics departed thither on the errand of salvation, and found still living an aged Hottentot woman, named Magdalena, who had been baptized by Schmidt, and who received them with some vague sensations of joy. On being questioned as to her recollections of Schmidt, she could recall little or nothing. She had become enfeebled by extreme old age, and the scenes of the early mission had passed from her memory. She could, however, bring to mind the description that had been given her of the suffering Saviour, who had died for her, and, after succeeding interviews with the new missionaries, she reawakened within herself many former impressions. She lived eight years after that event, once more confirmed in her Christian faith.

Among the North American Indians the missionary enterprise has met with less marked success. For a long time these missions were maintained in Georgia, among the Cherokees, and prosecuted in their new homes within the Indian territories, where they are yet conducted on a limited scale.

Another ancient scene of labor is the Fairfield mission in Canada West, which is still upheld, with rather feeble results, and from the nomadic character of our red men in general, no abiding influences can be expected from the introduction of Christianity, or success on a large scale awaited.

In reviewing the whole subject of the missionary obligation and its fulfillment throughout the long course of its past history, we must not overlook the remarkable instances of self-sacrifice exhibited among these early martyrs, in enduring a separation from their children. They were taken from their arms at ages varying from three to eight years, and sent to the German and American boarding-schools to be educated, and, in most cases, when the next interview took place between parent and child, neither could recognize the other.

This system, unnatural as it may seem to us of a less pure and an egotistic age, when self-sacrifice, as enjoined by the religion of Christ, is even held in disrepute, indicates the high purpose of the old Moravian's aspirations. A sacrifice that can overlook the claims of kindred, probably the strongest ties that exist in man, tearing away self from those earthly endearments for the sake of communicating to heathen the consolations of that faith which they regarded in the light of absolute knowledge, must be regarded as one of the finest exhibitions of the people whose life and history I have attempted to describe.

The world has seen its crusades, when thousands have gone forth on the mission of recovering the holy tomb, and become martyrs to a romantic and vain pursuit, with no end in view, save that of an empty ambition of acquiring a worldly renown. But in studying the memoirs of the earlier Moravian apostles, we shall find that, although a seeming spirit of adventure may have sent them forth, yet a serious religious purpose supported them under all difficulties, and that when once engaged in the work they had assumed, they devoted themselves sedulously to it to the last moment of their lives.

Among the pioneers of the Moravian heathen mission, there might be numbered Count Zinzendorf himself, who left the courts of Europe and engaged in the task of introducing Christianity among our aboriginal tribes, where we have seen him both on the West Indian plantations, and in the Indian wigwams of Pennsylvania and Connecticut, sitting face to face with those savages whom he wished to make his brethren.

The greatest contrasts of climate seem no obstacle to the missionary, who comes and goes from one extreme point of the habitable earth to the other, who passes from excessive heat to excessive cold, from the tropics to the arctic regions, under circumstances of mental and physical endurance, such as are seldom found on record. Of the hosts who have encountered such toils and trials many have died at their posts, victims to the climate of that flowery land where the air breathes, along with its spices, disease and death. Others have returned to their native country, or not unfrequently to Bethlehem and Nazareth, to enjoy the remnant of their days in quiet and repose. Here their labor of life is ended, and binding up the wounds it has inflicted, and soothing them with the solace of that benevolence which they find at all hands a voluntary offering, they await the final call to the world of the future, the visions of which have been prefigured in the hymns and anthems so often heard.

XVI.

SOCIAL AND PERSONAL CHARACTERISTICS.

From the peculiar cultus, the festive modes of life, and, above all, the rigid regulations in reference to age and sex, which governed every Moravian community, we may look for marked peculiarities of social and personal character.

Human love, we know, with all its joys and sorrows, forms one of the great pivots of society—giving employment to its hours, food for its thoughts, themes for its poesy, and causes for its tragedies; raising men and women to regions of bliss, and casting them down into the abodes of torture and despair; being the beginning, the middle, and the end of the individual's career, after he has taken his position in society, and we may therefore reasonably inquire how that same human passion figured in the little Moravian village.

In more primitive times during the momentous epoch termed courtship, it was unusual for the fair lady to have seen her intended spouse even a single time previous to the betrothal, and all the preliminaries of an event on which the heart hangs its entire destiny became the work of a day. Both clergy and laity submitted the decision of their connubial choice to the lot, evincing, by this mode of procedure, an entire submission to the will of the Lord, and employing this touchstone of spiritual faith in every important and decisive step. With regard to the merit of this singular feature of Moravianism, much discussion has arisen, but in the adoption of such a pure and devotional principle, and its application to the ventures of life, which the world generally regards as under the control of an unknown fate, we discover evidences of a high order of Christianity. It was the genius of Moravianism to submit all decisions to a supreme will and direction, and, in so doing, the lot was the most available agent. In this manner, self-sacrifice was an offering, and as the passions gave way to a sense of duty the soul hastened forward in the paths and pursuits of Christian hope.

There was, however, another tribunal, into whose presence the important question had to be brought before an espousal could be ratified, and that was the Elders' Conference. The sanction of this body was required in all cases of proposal between the future man and wife, and the dread suspense that preceded this conference formed an important passage in the history of love. The avenue I have described as leading from Herrnhut to Berthelsdorf, the seat of the conference, was a path of sighs to many of those disconsolate ones who returned over it homeward with a negative reply.

Yet it is not to be supposed that these matrimonial regulations shut out from the Moravian all the reciprocities of the sexes that are wont to precede an espousal. The loves of the unmarried had many an interesting and imaginative episode, and passed through the various crises of fear and hope, disappointment and realization, that, all the world over, characterize the oft-told story of the tender passion. As long as humanity lasts, the well-known history of human loves will be enacted again and again, and under every form of exterior life, the same sentiments will reveal themselves.

Under the old Moravian code, in cases where the affections were early placed, and human arbitrament was deemed sufficient, the decision by lot was often evaded. In such cases, the romance of courtship usually led to a suspension from the rights and privileges of the particular congregation where the infringing parties resided, and they were desired to remove without its pale, and were no longer considered members.

To rescue these tales of the past, evincing the all-conquering power of mutual love and affection over the ordinances of the church, is not my province; yet I refer to them as some of the curious reminiscences of an age of simple and hardy faith. When the maiden Sister in those times was an inmate of the "Sisters' House," access to her presence was an insuperable difficulty; the name and claims of her suitor were not unfrequently made known to her, and an acceptance or refusal decided upon after some subsequent interviews at home. As to the results of such unions, many were fortunate and happy, while, on the other hand, some injudicious espousals never yielded to the moulding hand of time, and that which was uncongenial in our nature remained so until death unlinked the chain. Upon the whole, however, the Moravian marriage was productive of the average sum of good that characterizes the ordinary tenor of connubial life, and it can scarcely be said that the singularity of form in the choice of husband and wife led to more unhappy alliances, than we see in the daily drama of human love and passion.

In this aspect of modern society, the springs of misfortune and sorrow generally flow from the disappointed ambitions and the thwarted purposes of worldly life, the jealousies, the hatreds and the rivalries of false pride, and the worship of self. In the community, which I here present to the reader, there were few struggles of selfish ambition, and as both partners were pledged to one spiritual purpose, a pure and holy marriage came on apace, and, long ere the close of a well-spent career, ripened into a more than earthly love. In our view of society at large, we shall find that the antecedents of marriage are, in but few cases, an earnest of continued felicity in its subsequent stages, and that when beauty, fortune, and impassioned declarations add to the romance of courtship, they in most instances but serve to darken the shadows that fall upon the scenes of a commonplace existence, after reality has made its revelations of the weaknesses that mutually exist. The old Moravian courtship, therefore, detracted but little from the aggregate of a happy life, and we may justly regard that feature as in perfect keeping with all its other forms of pure devotion and spiritual motive.

As regards the modeling of characters, we can look for few finished specimens of accomplishment, taking the word in its usual and conventional force. But if we assume a chaste Christian tone and modest demeanor as the highest requisite of womanly and manly worth, many examples can be pointed out in all Moravian circles. This tone we find to be a result of those influences which point directly to an emotional education. High intellect, wherever it exists, being brought into the service of the heart, all the gifts of mind being employed as the mere instruments of devotion, the life of the model Moravian retains its own peculiar cast. Its modest refinement of Christian thought could not easily be entered into by people of a worldly intellectuality, whose natures are expanded into a wider and colder philosophy, who worship man, as he is seen every day, who never form an ideal that ranks above some showy image of humanity, or who never allow that ideal to go beyond the reach of mere intellect. In Germany, where the standard of a literary and musical education is infinitely higher than here, specimens of the cultivated woman are more frequent than among us. At various periods of its history, Moravianism was embraced by noble families, and others of prominent rank in European society, the descendants of whom still hold to the primitive faith and institutions of Herrnhut, and use the phraseology of Zinzendorf.

In addition to those who have come within the scope of these sketches, there have been handed down to us the names of many remarkable women who were exemplary and distinguished in their day, and who, by their poetical talents, added to the lyrics of the church. The cultus of the Moravian, as already shown, is essentially poetical, and its exercise cannot but impart a bias to the female character, which reflects all the beauties of the poetry of religion. The imagery of such a Christian creed is pure and simple, and addresses itself with distinctive force to the sensibilities of the female heart, and we may not wonder, therefore, if a refined, spiritual impress, even if high intellectual culture be wanting, should distinguish the portraiture of Moravian women.

It may be worthy of mention, as one of the curiosities of literature, that Goethe formed an early and Platonic acquaintance with a Moravian Sister of Herrnhut, and in his "Wilhelm Meister" furnishes a synopsis of her life and character, in the ideal he has there presented under the "Confessions of a Beautiful Soul." At the period when he was drawn toward Moravianism, the society was advanced in form and thought, and attached to itself many intellectual minds. In the idealistic picture alluded to he has portrayed, with a masterly hand and with the most minute touches of a psychological artist, the inner history of a female soul, of one who was supposed to be gifted with all the delicate perceptions of a refined religion.

In the "Confessions" of this remarkable being, she acknowledges the Moravian belief and cultus as the nearest approach to her own preconceptions and the goal of that true sympathetic feeling she had long been striving after. The great poet subjects his type of female spiritual beauty to a wonderful analysis of self-examination and experience, and as she is allowed to narrate her own mental history, she holds up to view, with marvelous distinctness, every phase in the gradation from a worldly and a commonplace to a religious felicity, viewed in those lights which a Moravian cultus imparts.

The countenance itself of many distinguished personages of our church is a most striking interpreter of the ruling characteristic disposition, and inward intelligence of him or her whom it represents. Thus in the lineaments of Count Zinzendorf, Anna Nitschmann, Christian David, Spangenberg, Christian Renatus von Zinzendorf, James Hutton, Heckewelder, and in the large gallery of Moravian portraits, we find the whole sum of human benignity expressed, and this pictorial exponent tells us, as well as their written history, that their mission was one of love to mankind.

The simplicity of costume common to those days served to cast in still stronger light the pure expression of the outward person. The dress of the women was not less marked for its simplicity than that of the men, and the cap, with its Choir ribbon, the simple handkerchief thrown across the shoulders and primly drawn together in front, rendered the unpretending figure as morally attractive and as spiritually noble as can be found among the ideal images which art borrows from the exaggerations of history and poetry. Although the type of the "Sister" in attire, physiognomic expression, and Moravian feeling and phraseology, is scarcely to be found among us at this day, yet it is frequent in all our European communities, and but little modified by the influences of surrounding society.

In forming an estimate of character, as exhibited among the people of these communities, we must study the German temperament itself, from which its chief elements are derived. The "gemüthlichkeit" of that nation is found to address us in all the productions of art, and in all the forms of religion. The proper rendering of this term is, the expression of mind educated by heart. Both in man and woman do we see the significance of this phrase. It admits access from one individual to the other by a ready process, and once drawn to him, he is held by a tenacious grasp. The passion of the Teutonic race pervades all the manifestations of human thought, whether it belong to fiction, poetry, painting, the love of music, or the externals of church worship. This nationality of temperament is carried by the German Moravian to his adopted country, and hence we find among that people in this country many of those peculiarities and amiabilities of social character which spring out of the old Teutonic nature.

Our relations with the parent country are becoming more and more relaxed, and the scions of American growth are prone to throw off all the associations of German extraction, so that as a purely American Moravianism takes the place of the German school of faith and manners, much is lost in the essential forms, and the warmth of the primitive worship is largely diminished. I will not pretend to say that the practices of Christian worship in closest affinity with American life are less sincere, or that their religion is less true, yet, from the picture hitherto presented of the lively and cheerful cultus of the Moravian, Christianity comes up before us in attitudes seldom, if ever, elsewhere presented.

That the Moravian mode could be placed before society to imitate, we know is entirely impracticable, and the doubtfulness of such an application becomes more and more evident as the age develops its character for luxury and externality. Those naïve enjoyments, which were interwoven with the religious practices of the Moravian, necessarily implied a forbearance of ostentation and a "contentment with little." Out of this grade of human life, at all times and among all people, the chief sum of positive religious feeling proceeds, and the moment that society rises into luxury and stern conventional forms, that element subsides. In other words, the grade of social life wherein the heart rules is entitled to be called the model life of humanity, and the farther we diverge from it, the farther we recede from the true destiny of our earthly existence. As already said, I would not pretend to advocate all the forms of Moravian life at this advanced period of society, and in what it supposes itself to be, a high state of outward refinement, or recommend their application to the religion of the age; yet many things which have been laid aside, as the useless symbolism of a past generation, could be revived to beautify our worship and render it more captivating to that large number who, as they are carried down the tide of time, are steadily steering out of the way of its influences.

Under the frequent use of the term poetry, as applied to the Moravian worship, I do not wish to detract from its value or import; since, next to religion itself, nothing on earth is purer, nor can the soul be more readily admitted into its sacred depths than through these passages from an outer to an inner life.

XVII.

WILLIAM HENRY VAN VLECK.

Of all the noted men and women, whose names have been associated with the events and identified with the institutions of the Moravian Church, none belonging to this country have, as yet, come under our notice. Nearly all the personages of those early times were emigrants from Europe, who, in carrying out the great task assigned them, had to compass sea and land, forsake home and kindred, sacrifice fortune and the advantages of birth and social position. To their posterity they left a new sphere of activity. The church, which had been planted and nurtured into a growth of fair proportions, exhibiting its ripening fruits, was to be preserved in flourishing beauty, and guarded from internal decay. Among the many eminent divines who have thus contributed to the perpetuation of Zinzendorfian life and spirit among us, no one more than William Henry Van Vleck, deserves to be held in sacred remembrance. Born in Bethlehem, in 1790, he was placed at the usual age in Nazareth Hall, where he afterwards entered upon a course of theological study, and, upon its completion, went through the trials of a seven years' tutorship in that ancient seat of learning. Residing for a short time in Bethlehem as the spiritual adviser of the Brethren there, he was next called to take charge of the Philadelphia congregation. Previous to assuming this responsibility, he was united in marriage to Anna Eliza Kampman, who still survives him. Five years were usefully spent as the pastor of the Philadelphia church of the Moravians, when he received an appointment as Principal or Inspector of Nazareth Hall. On his arrival there, he found the school in a somewhat feeble condition, but, by judicious management and personal address, he succeeded, after a year's administration, in resuscitating it.

His next field of ministration was New York City, where he resided a few years, and then receiving episcopal ordination at Bethlehem, he removed to Salem, North Carolina, in order to officiate as pastor there, and, finally, to Bethlehem, where until near the last days of his life he exercised the functions of his sacred office. He delivered his final sermon on the 16th January, 1853, and expired on the nineteenth of the same month, at the age of sixty-two years.

During his pastoral career in Philadelphia, he was known and distinguished for that remarkable simplicity and unobtrusive demeanor that always marked his character, and made him, as a companion of the social circle, a welcome guest wherever he went. The species of Christian blandness found in him was its own peculiar and original type, adopting no conventional pattern, but aiming at the one great ideal of humanity,—man walking after and imbued with the spirit of Christ. His discourse in the pulpit partook of that soft, winning, and persuasive eloquence which seeks no *ad captandum* arguments to seize upon an auditory, but secures its attention by what is often termed a magnetic influence. In his language he borrowed freely from Holy Writ, but rarely to such an extent as to mar the propriety of his style. He lived altogether a gospel life, and hence was ever ready to quote appropriate passages. To him it was a delightful enjoyment to give a scriptural expression to all his views of surrounding existence, or add to its whole outer surface the glorious imaginings of an inner one. His style of preaching was of the order termed evangelical,—pure, simple, and scriptural.

The audience of a modern Christianity looks for polished language, imaginative conception, and all the accessories of rhetoric. Its attention must be drawn by intellectual display, and to secure a large and popular one, the preacher must call in the aid of much thought, and that thought constantly stripped of its old, and ever putting on some new dress, and gaining some new exuberance. But in the themes of our Moravian forefathers, erudition was laid aside, and the hearts of the hearers were only appealed to and approached by the repetition of the same language, the same emotional phraseology, which they received as children of a larger growth, and thus was constituted the true and only Herrnhutian church the world has ever seen.

Our American Bishop Van Vleck was distinguished by much of this fervid and artless eloquence, although modified by the language in which he generally addressed his people, and adapting itself to an age of new things, and to a people differing from those of the middle of the last century. Yet the doctrine of the cross underlay all this new exterior of modern thought, and the poetry which he frequently applied, in common with Zinzendorf and Spangenberg, although emanating from a different school of composition, flowed from the same fountain of inspiration. But the evangelical discourse, like the hymn or the melody sung from infancy to old age, never tires upon an audience who assemble for the purpose of listening to what it already knows and has heard. The most intellectual teacher of our time will become dull, his mental riches will be exhausted, and his audience will go in search of some other novelty; but the simple Christian discourse always remains fresh when the hearers to whom it is addressed judge it by the heart and not by the understanding.[1] If the

[1] It is not to be inferred from these remarks that all Moravian discourses are emanations of uneducated and merely emotional minds. Most of our German, and not a few among our American divines, are men of erudition and fine classical training; yet they constantly avoid a departure into the regions of polemics or the discussions of every-day life, and

occasion seemed to chime with his own feelings, the Bishop's quiet, soothing pathos and his simple lan-

---

they rarely contaminate the guileless subject of the cross with that irrelevant combination of moral, social, and political disquisition at which modern pulpit oratory aims, and which is craved by an audience who repair to the place of worship for the purposes of an intellectual repast. In appropriating the phrase, Evangelical preaching, to the language, thoughts, and usual vein of Moravian discourse, no proper conception of its peculiarity will be afforded.

The subject of the present sketch was remarkable for his powers of familiar exhortation; and on the eve of his departure from Herrnhut, he delivered to the Widows' Choir one of the most pleasing, impressive, and simple addresses that had ever been listened to. In his calm and quiet way, and in the garb of an unadorned language, the speaker is here seen to descend, like Zinzendorf in his communications with children, to the condition of human feelings nearest to nature; Christ becomes an invisible member of the spiritually-minded company, and participates in all its individual thoughts and desires. This is, therefore, not merely an evangelical mode of inculcation, but it might more properly be termed the Zinzendorfian form of evangelical discourse.

Among a number of cotemporaries of Bishop Van Vleck, I might name Lewis D. de Schweinitz, a descendant of Count Zinzendorf, as a man of great oratorical ability, and as fluent a master of words in prose as his ancestor was in poetical improvisation. He was equally at home in the German and the English tongues, giving utterance to all the impulses of the older school of Moravianism in the style of thought that characterized the German mind in contradistinction to that of the American. His profusion of gospel language and illustration drew toward him the admiration and esteem of his friend and companion Van Vleck, who not only studied him guage, were beautiful in the extreme, and in one of those solemn Moravian funerals, which I have had occasion to describe, his address always commanded the profound attention and moved the sensibilities of his hearers. For that which is usually termed pulpit oratory, he was, perhaps, nowhere more distinguished than when he resided in Philadelphia, where he flourished in the first stage of his clerical career, and was vigorous, and, at times, animated. His congregation was appreciative and much endeared to him.

---

as a model of eloquence, but loved him for the deep earnestness and sincerity of his nature. In the capacity of preacher, the Rev. Mr. de Schweinitz was chiefly known within the limits of the Brethren's society, but as a naturalist in the department of Flora, his name stood second to no other in the whole world of science.

At the same time, and in the same clerical circle at Bethlehem, lived Bishop Anders. He was a man of rare classical endowments, cultivated musical taste and ability, and conspicuous for his well-digested composition and powers of true eloquence in the pulpit. It may be added, in reference to the character of all these men, and particularly the details of familiar intercourse among the German Brethren, from Zinzendorf himself down to this time, that geniality, candor, good humor, confidence, and affection, were always depicted in the action, tone, and language of the group of friends. The Brethren, after long absence, always embraced and kissed each other, and the custom is upheld to this day among a portion of the elder Moravians. These characteristics, a reflection of the Christianity which was brought hither from Lusatia, impart a rich glow to the retrospect of Moravian life, and much of it can yet be seen wherever old influences are in operation.

In his later years, at Bethlehem, he preserved all the characteristics of his early eloquence, but it was more subdued, and his tone and language pointed to the sunset of life. His head now was gray, his features, never fair, bespoke the venerable bishop, and addressed you by the medium of that spirituality that always atones for the absence of physical beauty.

Owing to his singleness of purpose in evangelical pursuits, William Henry Van Vleck lived a steady and equable life. He was never flattered, nor was the purity of his faith weakened by an overweening popularity, yet the esteem in which he was held was great, and, what can scarcely ever be said of a man of note, his enemies, if he had any, were few. From the fineness of his organization proceeded that tenderness, forbearance, and deference in discussion which led him, as far as was consistent with personal judgment, to enter into the views of others by omitting self. And although subject to the ordinary infirmities of man, these were rarely seen to blemish the pure Christian model he presented to the world. To gain love, he accommodated himself to all with whom he came in contact, and such was the perfection of this "Disciple," that although he possessed a keen sense of the ridiculous, he showed no disposition to ridicule any of his fellow-men; for, with him, the faculty which is apt to give rise to the burlesque, was wont, in his gayer moments, to find its application in the heart, and instead of calling forth derision, excited sympathy. When he looked upon nature, its beauty received a spiritual interpretation, and that which constitutes the material element in its groupings and forms, became to him a thing of heaven, a typical loveliness. When he looked over the landscape and saw the country chapel standing there, he would say that it made the wilderness "bloom and blossom as the rose." All the grandeur and sublimity of the natural world, with him, retreated from mind and imagination back to the heart, and became a matter of adoration. He knew Art and felt her influences, and practiced in her temple; but even there he made a sacred application of all he learned, and drew consolation therefrom for his soul's nutriment.

If we were to institute a comparison between the two remarkable men whose lives we have reviewed, and our own remarkable Van Vleck, there might be found some striking points of resemblance.

In those two Germans, vigorous and sanguine temperaments imparted buoyancy to thought, and lighted up with cheerfulness all the phases of their apostolic career. Our American bishop was of an opposite temperament, and mostly cheered himself, after undue exertion, by rallying his powers and striving for a mastery over the despondency of a physically weak nature. Yet from this sensitive organization sprung many of those elements of character we find in Zinzendorf and Spangenberg. Being nurtured in the German language equally with the English, his

Moravianism was as essentially German as theirs, and as it formed a part of his family education to think in the phraseology of Herrnhut, all his feelings and associations partook of the old German Moravian nature. He was so well fitted to address a German audience by this medium, that, in his visit to Herrnhut in 1848, when he held a discourse there in the venerable church, he was listened to with intense admiration. His words, as they fell from his lips, were taken down by reporters and published next day, and many met him in the streets and thanked him for his delightful precepts.

Like those eminent Germans, he was always at prayer, and that which forms the greatest riddle to the philosopher, to discover why and how man should seek a power without his own mind, was to him a problem long and clearly solved. His communion, night and day, was with the Saviour, and all the terms of Zinzendorf and all the hymns he sung were at his command, and were the source of his highest enjoyment. Although his voyage of life was more serene than that of the illustrious founders of the modern church, yet his activity in his own sphere was equally great. The mission of their lives was to organize and originate, to govern, lead, and direct the people under their charge. Our own Van Vleck was born in a time when the whole institution had been tested and had lived and grown venerable through a century's trials and vicissitudes. His endeavors, therefore, were directed to conservative ends, and to an adherence to the past in its forms, its rituals, and simplicity of life.

Of all the personages of the Church of the Moravian Brethren, it would be difficult to find one so specially distinguished by that Christian gentleness that seemed to be attained by the subject of this sketch. Upon his visit to Herrnhut, in 1848, his fame had preceded him, and he was known and held in esteem there long before he had been welcomed by its people. Neither is it easy to copy such men as have been formed in the mould of William Henry Van Vleck, since his type of Christian beauty is extremely rare, and those forms of humanity that are fashioned after Christ are so marred by passions, so given to the conventionalities of a false standard of society, so led astray by the impulses of self, or so inflated by egotism, that a perfect model is vainly sought for. When man approaches nearest to all the Christian requirements, he is regarded as a wonder, as living above the ordinary atmosphere of human weakness and imbecility, and if he pursues a consistent career, with no gross errors to sully his history, he passes off from the stage of the living with a canonized reputation.

In the performance of his obsequies, the ceremonies which distinguish every Moravian funeral were observed, and he was carried to his place of earthly repose over the path that leads from the

Bethlehem Church to its cemetery, amid the notes of the dirge and the silent sympathy of a large body of friends, who, in the discharge of those last duties, performed to the many good who had preceded him, afterwards met in the hall of worship to crown the ceremony in the exercise of that melancholy joy, a Love-Feast.

THE END.

ERRATA.

Page 25, line 22.	*For* Wittemberg *read* Wittenberg.
" 31, " 22.	" tile-stone *read* tile-stove.
" 45, " 13.	*After* christianity *insert* of labor.
" 85, " 26.	*For* music *read* muse.
" 88, " 25.	" adopted *read* adapted.
" 89, " 28.	" Schrauterbach *read* Schrautenbach.
" 102, " 4.	" Halleasians *read* Hallensians.
" 111, " 25.	" South Carolina *read* North Carolina.
" 118, " 19.	" 1768 *read* 1760.
" 165, " 27.	" Great Sabbath *read* Good Friday.
" 180, " 15.	" practical *read* poetical.
" 185, " 2.	" cause *read* course.
" 196, " 28.	" youthful amateurs *read* early amateurs.
" 219, " 1.	" lived *read* live.
" 219, " 13.	" large *read* small.

www.ingramcontent.com/pod-product-compliance
Lightning Source LLC
LaVergne TN
LVHW020229110826
845151LV00003B/874

9781425531218